James Elliot

Moses and Modern Science

James Elliot

Moses and Modern Science

ISBN/EAN: 9783741163623

Manufactured in Europe, USA, Canada, Australia, Japa

Cover: Foto ©Thomas Meinert / pixelio.de

Manufactured and distributed by brebook publishing software
(www.brebook.com)

James Elliot

Moses and Modern Science

MOSES

AND

MODERN SCIENCE.

By JAMES ELLIOT,

FORMERLY PROFESSOR OF MATHEMATICS IN QUEEN'S COLLEGE, LIVERPOOL.

'Prove all things: hold fast that which is good.'—1 THESS. v. 21.

LONDON:
HODDER & STOUGHTON, 27, PATERNOSTER ROW.
1871.

MOSES AND MODERN SCIENCE.

INTRODUCTION.

IF we make our first approach to the Bible on
the side of the Old Testament, we see much
that looks to us, at first sight, unlike what we
might expect to find in a volume given to us
by divine inspiration. We meet, at the very outset, with an account of the creation of the world
which seems to be essentially at variance with
modern science, and of an apparently universal
deluge which the philosophy of the present day declares to have been impossible ; we encounter a
chronology which does not leave room for the
peopling of the world with those multitudes of men
which must have existed at certain given periods, or
for the succession of national and of natural changes
which archæologists and geologists assert to have
taken place since man first appeared on earth ; we
find a history which, according to our fallible judgment, falls beneath the dignity of inspiration in some

A

of its *apparently* unimportant details, and these sometimes expressed in terms such as we can hardly
suppose the Holy Spirit to have dictated; we occasionally detect particular numbers irreconcilable
with each other and with the probabilities of history;
we seem to have a spirit of war, hatred of enemies,
and revenge, rather than of peace and charity, per-
vading certain portions of some of the books, and a
narrative of actual wars carried on to the extent of the
extermination of whole nations,—men, women, and
children,—under the sanction of the Almighty himself; and, finally, we meet with instances of acts not
unlike those of fraud, treachery, or cruelty related
in such a way that *we might suppose them* to be professedly sanctioned, or at all events not condemned.

If, however, we are first introduced to the Bible
through the New Testament, we enter upon a scene
of a different aspect. In it we behold a code of morals
sublime in its purity; fraud, violence, and revenge entirely forbidden; pacific principles inculcated to the
extent of our seeking the good of all men, of no less
than loving our enemies, and of not even resisting
evil. In it we behold a wonderful scheme displayed,
such as it could never have entered into the mind of
man to conceive—of reconciling mercy with justice,
of uniting hatred to sin with pardon to the sinner,
and of restoring fallen man to communion with his
all-holy Creator. In it we have the most wonderful

history that has ever been written—of the Son of
God descending from the glories of heaven, taking
our humble nature upon him, passing through a life
incident to all the sufferings and even to the trials
of humanity, going about continually doing good,
labouring for the restoration of fallen men, perform-
ing wonderful miracles either in attestation of his
divine character or in manifestation of his compas-
sion for human sufferers, and ultimately dying a
cruel death on the cross, and, in the course of the
third day, rising from the grave as the first fruit of
a general resurrection. We have all these things
related, not in the most accurately grammatical
language (as, indeed, we have no reason to expect
from men of humble life, and writing also in a foreign
tongue), nor yet with the slightest tinge of the
misty and bombastic style into which men in their
position of life would inevitably have fallen in describing events so wonderful, if they had been de-
ceivers or even deceived, but in language of such
unembellished simplicity and dignity, as to bear upon
it an outward stamp of honesty and veracity, and
consequently, under the circumstances, of truth.
Nothing could account for such a style on such a
subject unless divine guidance.

Why, then, should we not receive the New Testament and reject the Old? We cannot do so for
several reasons:—*First,* from the high religious and

moral tone which, notwithstanding what has been said before, runs through the latter, and which, if in some respects behind that of the New Testament, is yet amazingly superior to that which pervaded all the world at that time, except that one nation to whom the books were given, and not excepting the whole of that nation, or even at times the greater part of it. *Second,* because it is, to a great extent, written in the same style of simplicity, dignity, and authority which we find to pervade the New Testament, rising occasionally to the highest flights of poetical sublimity and of moral grandeur. *Third,* because it is so entirely free from the childish superstitions and absurd stories which have always made their way into other books professedly describing events regarded as supernatural. *Fourth,* because the Old Testament contains many prophecies of events which could not have been foreseen by human sagacity, especially at the time at which they are known to have been written, and which yet were undoubtedly fulfilled. The *fifth* and last reason is, because several of the books of the Old Testament are referred to and occasionally quoted by our Saviour himself, who at the same time declares that they testify of him, and almost all of them by the apostles,—being so referred to and quoted by them as of divine authority.

We are therefore bound to return again to the Old

Testament, and to re-examine it ; to subject the
'oppositions of science' to more rigorous investigation, with a view to their removal, if possible, or to re-
consider the passages against which such oppositions
have been directed, lest by any means we should
have misunderstood them ; to examine the numbers
on which the received chronology of the Bible rests,
lest some error should have crept into them in copy-
ing, especially since they differ from those of the
Septuagint, of the Samaritan text, and of the history
of Josephus ; to make due allowance for similar
sources of error in regard to other apparent discre-
pancies and difficulties, remembering that we have
before us the oldest books known ; and to consider
if some matters which seem to us trivial, may not
have had an importance which we do not at once
perceive,—if our objection to certain modes of expression may not rest upon the standard which varying
fashion has introduced in our own day,—and if we
could expect that the same high moral code which
our Saviour inculcated could reasonably have been
insisted upon before adequate motives could be
adduced to support it, motives resting on the love of
God as manifested by the life and death of his Son.
All this we are bound to do (if we receive the New
Testament), not with an eagerness to find fault and
condemn, such as is too often exhibited, but with
the respect which is due to authors who bear in their

hands the highest credentials from our Lord and his
apostles.

Then, as to the extermination of the nations of
Canaan, all objection is silenced when we are told
that it was done by the express order of the Almighty, who has an undoubted right to employ
either pestilence, famine, or war for the chastisement
of guilty nations; that the Canaanites had reached
a degree of iniquity beyond even that of other
heathen nations, fearful as that was.; and that, in all
probability, their utter extermination had become a
necessity.

It is nowhere, however, asserted in the New Testament that *every portion* of the books arranged together as the Old Testament must be received as
inspired, and incapable of containing errors of any
kind; for we know that some errors in words and
in numbers have crept in, in certain places, it may
be by the fallibility of copiers, and we cannot even
be sure that whole books may not have been inserted
unwarrantedly; for we know not on whose authority
they were first admitted as canonical, and there are
several that have no prophetic announcements to
testify to their inspiration, no profession of that in
themselves, no attestation from our Saviour or from
the New Testament writers, and no peculiarly high
moral or religious tone.[1]

[1] I allude particularly to the books of Ecclesiastes and Esther.

Neither can we rest on the often-quoted statement of Paul, asserting,[1] it is alleged, that all Scripture is given by inspiration of God : for this would be an assertion going far beyond that for which it is appealed to, since *all Scripture* means simply all the books that have ever been written ; and when Paul himself confines the word to a more limited sense, as he does in the preceding verse, he thinks it necessary to prefix the word *sacred.*[2] Our translators have, in that passage, inserted the word *is* twice ; but if we omit the first, and render the Greek καὶ into the English *also,* we probably have the apostle's precise meaning : 'All Scripture given by inspiration of God, is also profitable for instruction,' etc. We must not overstrain the testimony of the New Testament in favour of the Old ; and probably we cannot take the latter as a whole, but must allow each book to stand on its own merits and its own authority.[3]

We find, too, that Christ and his apostles do not always quote the Old Testament, as we have it now, with verbal accuracy, as if they regarded the substance as of more importance than the exact words ; and sometimes the apostles bring out a sense from the

[1] 2 Tim. iii. 16.   [2] Τὰ ἱερὰ γράμματα.

[3] In saying this, I regret to differ from many worthy men ; but our fortress is assaulted so strongly on all sides, that, if its defence is to be maintained, it is absolutely necessary to consider *how much* we must defend, and to see that, in the attempt to hold unnecessary outposts, we do not weaken our position.

original different from that which it outwardly bears, as if they had authority to throw a new light upon it There are many of the merely historical parts of the Old Testament, in which the writer may simply have been bound down to veracity of narrative without further inspiration ; and certain portions are apparently compilations from other documents, or abridgments of these,[1] and, whatever the originals may have been, not themselves altogether free from errors.

Still there are many parts of the Old Testament which must either have been inspired literally throughout, or cannot have been inspired at all ; such, for instance, as the prophecies, and the account of the creation of the universe.

The prophecies have often been illustrated and defended by writers of ability, whose arguments have never been efficiently assailed ; but, on the other hand, the writings of Moses, and especially his accounts of creation and the deluge, have had to sustain a formidable attack on all sides from the votaries of science, while no complete and adequate defence, as far as I am aware, has ever been made, and multitudes are now beginning to regard the defence as hopeless. On the Continent, in fact, the majority of the educated are not *beginning* to entertain such sentiments, but maintain that these

[1] I refer to the books of Chronicles.

narratives, along with the accounts of everything else that is recorded in the Bible as miraculous, are merely exploded myths.

To show that more may be said in defence of Moses' history than is usually believed, and *that* in strict accordance with the light derived from the most advanced discoveries of modern research, these pages are written as a first instalment. May the Almighty be pleased to aid the attempt, and to make it useful for clearing away difficulties from the minds of those who are willing to believe, and for establishing the truth, whatever that may be ; for, clearly, whatever is truth cannot be displeasing to our Creator, or in any way counteract his revealed will. In this volume I confine myself to the subject of *the Creation*, as recorded in the first chapter of Genesis ; but entertain the purpose, if this attempt should be in any degree successful, and if health and ability for the work be given, to proceed next to the consideration of *the Unity of the Human Race*, of *the Antiquity of Man*, and perhaps also of *the Deluge* and *the Dispersion of the Nations.*

In our childhood we peruse the account of creation given in the Bible, taking the time occupied in it as literally six days, and wonder that so great a work (although at that stage we little dream of its actual greatness) could be begun, carried on, and finished in so very short a period. When we pass from this

stage to the readings of science, and find geologists
demonstrating that, so far from the earth being the
work of a few days, it must have occupied, in the
mere changes which took place on its surface, many
millions of years, we at first entertain doubts regarding the demonstration, or rather disbelieve it altogether, fancying that shells, bones, and other fossils
may have been created, unconnected with previous
life, in the conditions and situations in which they
are now found, being in fact only the resemblances
of animal and vegetable productions. When we
abandon this idea, since it would have implied that
our Creator employed systematic deception, we find
ourselves at first confounded and perplexed, and are
henceforth separated into two parties. The one
party give up the Bible narrative as one of the
numerous fables in which antiquity abounded, and,
though unobjectionable as an innocent delusion of
childhood, yet not worth a moment's thought to a
modern philosopher. The other party, having been
previously convinced of the truth of Christianity,
and of the divine authority of the many references
to the Pentateuch in the New Testament, find that
they cannot discard the narrative so lightly, even if
they would. They are therefore compelled to search
for some mode of interpretation which may show it
to be, at all events, not contradictory to the knowledge derived from scientific discoveries. They

know that God has written both books, the book of
science and the book of revelation, and that these
cannot, unless we erroneously interpret one or both,
be contradictory to each other.

A plausible resolution of the difficulty was that
which was primarily propounded by Dr. Chalmers,
and afterwards supported by Dr. Buckland and
others,—namely, that the long geological periods
were concluded before the six days of Moses' account
began ; that the commencement of the latter period
found the earth reduced by some convulsion or series
of convulsions to a state of chaos and of darkness,
sun and stars being entirely hidden from view ; that
these six were our ordinary days of twenty-four hours
each, and that during these took place that succession of changes, and the new creation of plants and
of animals, described in the first chapter of Genesis ;
light, which had been for a time totally obscured, re-
appearing in the course of the first day, and the sun
once more shining upon the earth on the fourth.

But when a better knowledge was attained of the
fossil remains buried in our rocks, it was found that
many species of animals which have existed on the
earth contemporaneously with man, had also preceded him by many ages, so that there could not
have been a period immediately preceding his
appearance, in which the previously existing races
were wholly destroyed. In the words of an author

whom I shall have occasion frequently to quote,[1]—
'In consequence of that comparatively recent extension of geological fact in the direction of the later
systems and formations, through which we are led
to know that the present creation was not cut off
abruptly from the preceding one, but that, on the
contrary, it dovetailed into it at a thousand different
points, we are led also to know that any scheme of
reconciliation which would separate between the
recent and the extinct existences by a chaotic gulf
of death and darkness, is a scheme which no longer
meets the necessities of the case. Though perfectly
adequate forty years ago, it has been greatly out-
grown by the progress of geological discovery, and
is adequate no longer.'

To meet this difficulty the scheme of Dr. Pye
Smith was devised, which adopts that of Dr.
Chalmers in all respects but one. It supposes the
destruction of animal and vegetable life which preceded the six days of Moses' account, not to have
been universal in its extent, but to have been confined to a limited district. 'It may have extended,'
it is said (returning to the work last quoted[2]), 'over
only a few provinces of Central Asia, in which, when
all was life and light in other parts of the globe,

---

[1] Hugh Miller, in the *Testimony of the Rocks*, p. 122 of first
edition.

[2] *Ibid.* p. 131.

there reigned for a time only death and darkness, amid the welterings of a chaotic sea, which at the divine command was penetrated by light and occupied by dry land, and ultimately, ere the end of the creative week, became a centre in which certain plants and animals, and finally man himself, were created. And this scheme, by leaving the geologist in this country and elsewhere (save, mayhap, in some unknown Asiatic district) his unbroken series, certainly does not conflict with the facts educed by geologic discovery. It virtually removes Scripture altogether out of the field. I must confess, however, that on this and on some other accounts it has failed to satisfy me.' The solution, in fact, is so much like patchwork, so artificial, that it would never have been resorted to but from a supposed necessity—a necessity which we shall find does not now exist, although, at the time at which Dr. Smith's view was promulgated, it may have appeared to do so. If we adopt that solution, does not all the dignity, the sublimity, the importance, of Moses' narrative disappear? The theory would probably itself altogether disappear as soon as the geology of Asia came to be thoroughly investigated.

Mr. Miller, with his usual sagacity, abandons both these theories, and reverts to an older and simpler one, taking it up, and working it out as it had never been before. His view is this: that the six days of

Moses were six long periods of time, each extending perhaps over millions of years ; so long, indeed,
that three, or at most four of them, were alone
sufficient to include all the series of events dis-
closed by geologists.[1] Of the transactions of those
three or four days only, his last and greatest work,
the *Testimony of the Rocks*, professes to furnish any
account, giving no explanation of the others, unless
in the shape of some probably incorrect suggestions
regarding the early appearance of light so long
before the formation of the sun. To account for
these long periods being spoken of as days, each
with an evening and a morning, he supposed the
revelation of them to Moses to have been made in
six visions, each occupying the space of a day and
night.

Even those who reject entirely the narrative of
Genesis, are obliged to admit that three of the days
of creation mentioned in it agree, to a remarkable
extent, with the three corresponding periods of

[1] In his third lecture, in the *Testimony of the Rocks*, he says : 'I
find myself called on as a geologist to account for but three of the
six. Of the period during which light was created,—of the period
during which a firmament was made, to separate the waters from the
waters,—or of the period during which the two great lights of the
earth, with the other heavenly bodies, became visible from the earth's
surface, we need expect to find no record in the rocks' (p. 134). He
does afterwards, however, find some geological work for the fourth
day, for he says in his fourth lecture (p. 175) : 'For the intervening
or fourth day we have that wide space presented by the Permian and
the Triassic periods.'

geology ; and the coincidence, it will be found as we advance, is closer than they, or even Mr. Miller, were aware of.[1]

This agreement they attribute to some small amount of scientific knowledge on the part of the writer, whoever he was, accompanied by a great sagacity. But the coincidence is beyond anything that could easily be explained in that way.

Mr. Miller's views I regard as, in general, not only beautifully elucidated, but sound ; and to a certain extent I purpose to avail myself of them, but at the same time to complete his scheme by bringing forward astronomy to the aid of geology, and filling up the details of the omitted days partly from the one science, partly from the other. At the same time, I dismiss the hypothesis of a *visionary* revelation to Moses, as purely fanciful and altogether unnecessary,—I divide the earlier geological periods, considered as days, somewhat differently,—and I entirely avoid his forced and

[1] Mr. Goodwin (*Essays and Reviews*, p. 239) says : ' Now these facts do certainly tally to some extent with the Mosaic account, which represents fish and fowl as having been produced from the waters on the fifth day, reptiles and mammals from the earth on the sixth, and man as made last of all. The argument, however, is far from exact, as, according to geological evidence, reptiles would appear to have existed ages before birds and mammals, whereas the creation of birds is attributed to the fifth day, that of reptiles to the sixth.' The coincidence in the case of the third day he tacitly admits, and his exception regarding the fifth and sixth the reader of this volume will find is unwarranted.

awkward explanation of the creation of light before that of the sun, and of the absence of that luminary, as well as of the moon, until the fourth day.

To arrive at all this, I have recourse to the Nebular Hypothesis of Laplace ; one which, it is needless to say, was not devised for any such purpose as elucidating or supporting the statements of Moses.[1]   Neither had I any such view in first receiving that hypothesis as admissible ; for I felt myself almost compelled to do that on astronomical grounds alone, before I saw that it had any bearing on the subject before us, unless in *apparent* opposi-

[1] This volume was already completed, with the exception of a few alterations, principally in the notes, before I was aware that I had been anticipated in the attempt to use the nebular hypothesis in defence of the account of creation given by Moses. I had not then seen or heard of Dr. M'Caul's pamphlet entitled *Some Notes on the First Chapter of Genesis*, in which the same view is taken of Laplace's idea.   Dr. M'Caul, however, although many of his remarks are excellent, has not been happy in his distribution of the geological periods among the successive days of creation, assigning ' the whole of the primary, secondary, and tertiary formations, with all their products,' to the first two days, and consequently attributing the growth and life of all their varied flora and fauna to a period preceding the formation of the sun, the changes of seasons, and the distribution of climates among the different zones of the earth.   In consequence of this, he has thrown himself open to the severe criticism of Dr. M'Causland in the last edition of his *Sermons on Stones*. That writer's objections on this ground, however, do not in any way militate against the views which I have advanced, as I have otherwise distributed the geological periods ; and his remaining objections also have no weight, I think, against the modes of explanation which I have followed on other points.

tion to the account given in the Bible. Now I go
further, and regard Laplace's hypothesis as not
merely admissible, but almost unavoidable. It
explains all the remarkable coincidences in the
motions of the planets, is consistent with geological
deductions, and has not a single fact militating decidedly against it. Nothing could have prevented
its general reception, except its supposed atheistic
tendency. If its author had any such view, *that*
can form no objection to us, when we take the
weapon out of the hands of unbelievers and turn
it against themselves. Those who peruse the
following pages carefully, will, I think, admit that,
if my positions are found to be tenable, I have
established a closer agreement between the record
of Moses and the revelations of science than has
ever been suggested before; while all the arguments and the sarcasms launched against previous
interpretations lose their force, falling on empty '
air.

Still I am well aware of the difficulty of the task
set before me, and scarcely venture to hope that
my scheme will be found in all minor matters
faultless; but I trust that I have at least set up
the framework of a sound structure, which the
learning and the ingenuity of others may ultimately render more perfect in its details. I am,
no doubt, building on another man's foundations

and even more than that ; for I found Mr. Miller's edifice, with three of its six compartments, not only built, but almost perfect even in their decorations, with the fourth, however, unfinished, and with the remaining two only vaguely marked out. These two last I have attempted to erect from the foundation, disregarding my predecessor's design : the fourth I have endeavoured to complete, and to the other three—the three first mentioned—I have made some additions.[1]

Wherever I have availed myself of his labours, I have made free acknowledgment. If I be blamed for using these too liberally, I at least avoid thereby the reproach that has been thrown out against previous 'theological geologists,' of 'overthrowing one another's theories.' This has, indeed, been too often the case ; and there is some ground for the ridicule that has been cast upon so many ingenious cosmogonies which have never survived their own generation. Not only have they been constructed principally on hypotheses, but these hypotheses have been devised solely for the object in view. Hugh Miller's scheme, on the contrary, involves no hypothesis, but rests wholly on close induction ; and that which is now added to it,

---

[1] I had almost continued the metaphor by adding that I have removed the scaffolding and the centres which he had placed under his graceful arches after they were already raised, and have left them to stand by their own equilibrium.

although resting on a hypothesis, does not employ
one made up for the purpose, but one that was
originally suggested with a very different aim, by
one of the highest of mathematicians, and regarded
with respect by our ablest astronomers, on astronomical grounds alone,—a hypothesis, in fact, which
can hardly be dispensed with in its own depart-
ment.

The blunders of cosmogonists have arisen from
attempting to raise scientific systems on foundations merely religious, with little knowledge of
material philosophy, just as philosophers have fallen
into errors equally great from attempting to dictate
to religion from conclusions drawn only from science.
It is from scientific materials alone that science can
be built up, although, in building, religion must be
kept constantly in view, in order that we may construct nothing that is in flagrant, or even in probable,
opposition to its truths. So also it is from religious
materials alone that religious systems can be built
up or received, although science must meanwhile
be kept before us, lest we raise or adopt a religious system that is in opposition to it; for, as
said before, true religion and true science can never
conflict.

As the prophecies, not being intended to gratify
curiosity, can rarely be interpreted till they are
fulfilled, and many, attempting to lay down future

history from prophecy, have signally failed, and yet the prophecies of the Scriptures, when fulfilled, have often been shown to be consistent with the events, never to be inconsistent; *so* those portions of the sacred writings which encroach on the domain of science, not being intended to gratify mere scientific curiosity, cannot be made the instruments for constructing philosophical systems, and yet, when true philosophical knowledge is attained, it is often found to be consistent with the statements of revelation, never to be inconsistent. Those who endeavour to prove the harmony of the sacred records with the facts of philosophy ascertained by lawful modes of research, are never, as Mr. Miller remarks, to be confounded with those who, without that knowledge which can be acquired only from philosophical investigation, construct philosophical systems out of revelation.

Some there are, however, who say that all attempts such as I am now making are lost labour,—that the truth stands firm as a rock which no opposing efforts can shake,—and that all the assaults made upon it are frivolous and futile, and not worth while to oppose. The truth, no doubt, is as firm as a rock; but what is the truth? Let that be fairly established. Then, if the truth is firm, the minds of those that investigate it, and even of those that receive it, are not so firm; and it is well that faith should be strengthened by sound reasoning.[1] It is not the time to treat the assaults of science, even if falsely so called, with contempt. Daily the opponents of revealed religion come out and taunt us,[2] setting us at defiance ; and ought we weakly to decline their challenges? If we either treat them with disdainful silence, or fail to meet them effectually, the faith of some is weakened, and the minds of many waverers are turned the wrong way. It is our duty assuredly to contend for the truth with every fair weapon of argument.

I admit meeting with difficulties. Some of these have been very formidable ; but I have nowhere concealed or evaded them, and have, I trust, met them fairly, without anywhere overstraining my argument or introducing any forced interpretation. How far I have overcome them I leave my readers to judge. If I have sometimes been led to speak too confidently, I have to request that anything so said may be taken simply as the enunciation of a proposition which the reader may accept or not, accordingly as he may be satisfied with the demonstration or otherwise. The

---

[1] ' Who, when he was come, helped them much who had believed through grace ' (Acts xviii. 27).

[2] ' The current cosmogony is not only without a single fact to stand on, but is at variance with all our positive knowledge of nature.'— *Essays by Herbert Spencer*, 2d series ; Essay I, p. 55.

explanations I have advanced are often of so novel
a character, that I give them with hesitation.   I
expect opposition, and I shall welcome a fair discussion of them.

CHAPTER I.

THE FIRST DAY OF CREATION.

'In the beginning God created the heaven and the earth. And the earth was without form, and void; and darkness was upon the face of the deep: and the Spirit of God moved upon the face of the waters.' —GEN. I. 1, 2.

THE *Nebular Hypothesis*, originated by the genius of Laplace, supported by the numerous and excellent observations of Sir William Herschel,[1] if not primarily suggested by him, was long viewed with suspicion by the religious world, as giving an origin to the heavens and the earth

[1] 'Herschel, en observant les nébuleuses au moyen de ses puissans télescopes, a suivi les progrès de leur condensation, non sur une seule, ces progrès ne pouvant devenir sensibles pour nous qu' après des siècles; mais sur leur ensemble, comme l'on suit dans une vaste forêt l'accroissement des arbres, sur les individus de divers âges, qu'elle renferme. Il a d'abord observé la matière nébuleuse repandue en amas divers dans les différentes parties du ciel dont elle occupe une grande étendue. Il a vu dans quelques-uns de ces amas, cette matière faiblement condensée autour d'un ou de plusieurs noyaux peu brillans. Dans d'autres nébuleuses, ces noyaux brillent davantage relativement à la nébulosité qui les environne. Les atmosphères de chaque noyau, venant à se séparer par une condensation ultérieure, il en résulte des nébuleuses multiples formées de noyaux brillans très voisins et environnés, chacun, d'une atmosphère; quelquefois la matière nébuleuse, en se condensant d'une manière uniforme, produit

altogether different from that ascribed to them by Moses, and as, in fact, according to *their* idea, almost or altogether dispensing with a Creator; and, probably for the same reasons, it received a welcome from sceptical philosophers. Without that hypothesis, however, we can obtain no explanation whatever of the origin of certain remarkable coincidences in the motions of the planets. These are: 1. The orbits of all the planets, primary and secondary, are nearly circular.[1] 2. The planes of the orbits of all the primary planets (a few of the asteroids excepted), and of almost all the secondary, are coincident nearly with the plane of the ecliptic. 3. The sun's equator, and the equators of all the primary planets, as far as we know, are nearly in the same plane with each other, and with the planes

les nébuleuses que l'on nomme *planétaires.* Enfin, un plus grand degré de condensation transforme toutes ces nébuleuses en étoiles. Les nébuleuses, classées d'après cette vue philosophique, indiquent, avec une extrême vraisemblance, leur transformation future en étoiles, et l'état antérieur de nébulosité des étoiles existantes. Ainsi l'on descend, par le progrès de la condensation de la matière nébuleuse, a la considération du soleil environné autrefois d'une vaste atmosphère, —considération a laquelle je suis remonté par l'examen des phéno-mènes du système solaire. Une rencontre aussi remarquable, en suivant des routes opposées, donne à l'existence de cet état antérieur du soleil, une grande probabilité.'—*Exposition du Système du Monde,* par M. le Marquis de Laplace, liv. v. ch. vi.

[1] No doubt the laws of gravity and inertia together compel the planets to move in elliptic orbits; but, in as far as these two laws are concerned, the ellipses might have any extent of eccentricity, and would not necessarily approximate to circles.

of the orbits of these planets. 4. All the primary planets, and all the secondary, except two or three on the exterior verge of the system,[1] revolve in the same direction round the sun. 5. The sun and all the planets, as far as we know, rotate on their axes in the same direction, and that, too, in the direction of their annual revolutions.[2]

These remarkable coincidences cannot be the result of chance.[3] Neither can they be explained

[1] There are two, at least, of the satellites of Uranus, the same which form the exception to the second coincidence ; but these are not necessarily or probably two separate and independent exceptions. For if these satellites originally revolved in the plane of the ecliptic, and in the general direction, any disturbing force which turned their orbits more than ninety degrees from their original plane would also necessarily give them a retrograde motion.

[2] 'Quoique les élémens du système des planètes, soient arbitraires, cependant ils ont entre eux, des rapports qui pouvont nous éclairer sur son origine. En les considérant avec attention, on est étonné de voir toutes les planètes se mouvoir autour du soleil, d'occident en orient, et presque dans un même plan ; les satellites en mouvement autour de leurs planètes dans le même sens et à peu près dans le même plan que les planètes ; enfin, le soleil, les planètes et les satellites dont on a observé les mouvemens de rotation, tourner sur eux mêmes dans le sens et à peu près dans le plan de leurs mouvemens de projection.' —*Système du Monde*, liv. v. ch. vi. To these coincidences Laplace adds in Note vii : ' Le peu d'excentricité des orbes des planètes et de satellites.' I have not followed him in everything, because he was not aware of the exceptional cases ; and we are not now certain of the nature of the rotation of the satellites, except that of our own moon.

[3] 'Des phénomènes aussi extraordinaires ne sont point dus à des causes irrégulières. En soumettant au calcul leur probabilité, on trouve qu'il y a plus de deux cent mille milliards à parier contre un, qu'ils ne sont point l'effet du hasard ; ce qui forme une probabilité bien supérieure à celle de la plupart des événemens historiques dont

without the aid of the nebular hypothesis ; whereas,
if we receive that hypothesis, they all flow from it
as necessary consequences.[1]

Of course the Creator of the planets could have
imparted all their motions to them, and all their
peculiar coincidences, on their first formation, by
his immediate power, according to his sovereign
will ; and *that* he would have been the more likely
to do, if the same ends could not have been
attained by intermediate agency, since the greater
number of these coincidences are necessary, as
those eminent mathematicians, Laplace[2] and La-

nous ne doutons point. Nous devons donc croire, au moins avec la
même confiance qu'une cause primitive a dirigé les mouvemens
planétaires.—*Ibid.*

[1] Laplace also deduces from it other coincidences in the solar
system,—namely, that of the periods of rotation of our moon and of
the other satellites, with their periods of revolution round their
primaries ; and the extraordinary harmony presented by the three first
satellites of Jupiter, whose motions are so adjusted relatively to each
other, that the mean longitude of the first, minus three times that of
the second, plus twice that of the third, is invariably equal to 180
degrees. But his argument on these points is not so conclusive ; nor
is it necessary, for there is enough without it ; and the coincidence
of the periods of rotation and revolution of the satellites, our moon
excepted, is not well established. He also deduces from his hypothesis, as its natural result, the spheroidal form of the planets ; and
undoubtedly his is the simplest explanation, although there might
be some other *possible* ways in which that form might ultimately be
attained even by solid bodies rotating on their axes.

[2] ' Je suis parvenu a démontrer que, quelles-que soient les masses des
planètes, par cela seul qu'elles se meuvent toutes dans le même sens,
et dans des orbes peu excentriques et peu inclinés les uns aux autres ;
leurs inégalités sont periodiques et renfermées dans d'étroites limites,

grange,[1] have demonstrated, to ensure the stability
of the solar system.   But, as far as we see of our
all-wise Creator's mode of action in the government
of the material universe, we perceive that he always
prefers the employment of secondary causes for
the attainment of his purposes, when they can be
effected by means of these, rather than the direct
action of his own power ; and we also perceive that
coincidences and securities in other instances are
brought about not merely by the will of the
Almighty, but by means of some law from which
they emanate.   On the part of man, it is regarded
as a higher attainment when he makes a machine to
do his work, than when he does it himself ; and it
certainly does not detract from the praise which we

en sorte que le système planétaire ne fait qu' osciller autour d'un état
moyen dont il ne s'écarte jamais que d'une très petite quantité.'—
Système du Monde, liv. iv. ch. ii.

[1] ' We have spoken of certain constituent elements of our planetary
scheme,—as, for instance, the facts that the earth and its companions
move in orbits of but small eccentricity, that the inclinations of the
planes of their orbits are small, and that they revolve around our
luminary in one uniform direction.   Now it appeared to Lagrange
that the existence of such primal arrangements impresses upon the
effects of perturbation a condition which, in the happy phrase of Sir
John Herschel, may well be termed the *Magna Charta* of our system.
Subjecting the entire question, taken in its highest generality, to
treatment by his masterly and most penetrating analysis, Lagrange
discovered that all changes of the *essential* elements of any orbit which
can arise from perturbations must be periodical.'—*Cyclopædia of the
Physical Sciences*, by J. P. Nichol, LL.D., art. *Perturbations.*   If
any one thinks that the claims of these two great men are conflicting,
I leave it to others to reconcile them.

owe to our Creator's wisdom and power, to maintain that it is by means of the laws of gravitation
and inertia that he causes the planets to revolve
round the sun, and the satellites round their
primaries, in elliptic orbits, while he could have
done so, without either gravitation or inertia, by the
mere continued fiat of his will. In fact, it raises
far higher our perception of his greatness, when we
behold him educing so many harmonious and
beneficent results from the employment of these two
simple laws alone, than if we saw the same results
attained without the agency of any laws at all. In
like manner, when we see that the many remarkable
coincidences which we have already noticed in the
motions of the planets might all have arisen from
one simple cause, our conception of the wisdom
which could have originated the construction of so
glorious a system by means so little complex is
greatly exalted. To fancy, however, that the
original nebula could have produced itself, or could
have arisen by accident, or could have existed from
all eternity, would indeed be atheism.

No doubt, when we speak of secondary causes,
we are entirely ignorant of the way in which any
particular cause comes to be invariably followed by
a particular effect ; and when we say that certain
results are the consequences of certain laws of nature,
it may be that this in reality has no other meaning

than that the Almighty has thought good to confine himself, in the government of his creation, to certain modes of action to which we give the name of *laws*, and that these results are not brought about by any powers vested in the things themselves, but do in every case emanate from the direct action of the almighty power. Still, whatever may be the mode of explaining the connection of cause and effect, and the precise meaning of *general laws*, we know that God does in reality subject all his operations to these laws, unless in the case of miracles ; and if he had not done so, all nature would have been chaos *to us*, and the researches of philosophy would have been forbidden to us from their very commencement, or limited, as in the creed of the Mahometans, to the solitary explanation, 'God wills it.' Even in the cases of miracles, as recorded, it appears to be a general principle to employ secondary causes as far as they will go, using miraculous power as it were economically. Thus, when a passage was to be made for the Israelites through the Red Sea, we do not hear that God merely ordered the sea to stand aside to the right hand and to the left, but that 'the Lord caused the sea to go back *by a strong east wind* all that night.'

Seeing, then, that God conforms in all ordinary cases to the general laws which he has himself imposed upon creation, never deviates from those

laws unless for some great and important purpose,
and even in such deviations uses those laws as far
as they will go, it is only reasonable to conclude,
that in bringing about that wonderful group of
coincidences which has been detailed in the solar
system, he has brought them about by the agency of
some general law, and not by his mere sovereign will
independently of law. Otherwise, since they *might*
all have been the results of a general law, and would
have been its *natural* results, he would have assumed
an *appearance* of acting upon general principles when
he was not doing so, and would have misled the
researches of that very philosophy which his usual
mode of action tends to encourage and to assist ; for
God is not an enemy to philosophy, but the author
of it.

We can apply these general remarks, of course, to
our present subject, only if we can produce a hypothesis capable of accounting for those coincidences
on ordinary principles ; and if there is nothing un-
reasonable or extravagant about that hypothesis, we
are entitled to rest upon it as probably the true one.

The nebular hypothesis, then, is this,—in a form
slightly altered in minor points from that in which
it was originally propounded, but the same in all
essentials.

The whole solar system, consisting of sun, planets,
and satellites, is supposed to have been created in

the state of a cloud, or *nebula* of *dust* (as it has been called), made up of the separate atoms of which the various kinds of matter consist; in the words of a lucid expounder of the hypothesis,[1] 'a huge, dark, chaotic, void, and formless mass.' It is further supposed that these atoms attracted each other with forces proportional to their own weights, and inversely proportional to the squares of their distances from each other—unless in so far as that law may have been modified at infinitesimally small distances by specific attractions and repulsions among the different kinds of atoms—and that the whole cloud was not at rest, but with two motions originally given to it, one progressive, the other rotatory, just as it would have had (if we might venture to use such an expression) if it had been thrown carelessly out of the hand of its Creator. Finally, let it be added to our supposition, that the cloud was without sensible heat, but with latent heat everywhere diffused through it, or, according to the language of more recent science, with the power of having heat excited in it.[2]

[1] Professor Nichol, in the *Cyclopædia of the Physical Sciences,* art. *Nebular Hypothesis.*

[2] The modifications I have made in the original hypothesis rather tend to its simplification than otherwise. Laplace, although he sometimes speaks of *molecules,* seems rather to have regarded the original nebula as existing in a gaseous condition, 'à l'état de vapeurs,' and at a high temperature; whereas it seems to me a simpler supposition that the original state was that of solid atoms, entirely destitute of sensible

In this hypothesis, with the law of inertia super-added—which, as well as that of gravitation, is not hypothetical—we have enough not only to account for all the otherwise inexplicable coincidences with which we started, but to explain the origin of every movement and of every existing state of things in the solar system,[1] vegetable and animal life excepted.

Before going further, however, let us ask if any supposition could more clearly elucidate the words : ' In the beginning God created the heavens and the earth. And the earth was without form, and void ; and darkness was upon the face of the deep.' The earth was absolutely *without form*, regular or irregular, for it was not yet cut out from the great cloud of 'dust.' It was truly *void*, because, from the entire absence of heat, all the atoms were in a solid condition, with no gaseous matter to fill up the interstices, and consequently with every atom surrounded by a vacant space, boundless in extent compared with that of the atom within it. If the

heat, that heat being subsequently developed or produced by condensation of the mass.   I have also more distinctly defined the original endowment of the nebula with two distinct motions, as neither could have arisen subsequently from mutual attraction among the molecules. In this I agree with the view of Professor Nichol, as he has given it in his latest work already quoted, although he had previously expressed a different opinion.

[1] In this I do not include comets, which probably do not belong to our system.

nebula had extended only as far as the orbit of
Neptune, its density would have been less than
the two hundred millionth part of that of our
atmosphere at the level of the sea ; and it *must* have
extended beyond that distance: if twice as far, it
would be eight times more diffused. Finally, *darkness was upon the face of the deep*, because in a cold
so intense nothing whatever could be luminous, while
the sun itself was not yet in existence, but merely
the dark central portion of the nebula, from which
the sun was afterwards to be formed.

By the expression 'the deep,' readers of the Bible
usually entertain a vague idea that the *ocean* was
intended; and when they call to mind that there
was as yet no ocean, their ideas become more vague
still. But now they may have some conception of
its meaning, the least extent which we can reasonably attribute to the great nebula being twice the
diameter of the orbit of Neptune, or eleven thousand
millions of miles. What a depth! If our hypothesis is the true one, it supplies a wonderful com-
mentary on the words—*formless, void, dark, deep ;*
darkness absolute, and such a depth, such a vacancy,
and such a destitution of form, as it could not have
entered into the mind of man to conceive.

Ovid undoubtedly derived the groundwork of his
accounts of creation and the deluge, directly or in-
directly, from those of Moses, as well as some other

c

portions of his *Metamorphoses.*[1] Poetic fancy and sagacious conjecture have supplied the details, sometimes very happily. In his description of the first stage of creation, he comes wonderfully near to depicting that which the previous considerations would lead us to believe to have been the actual state of things:

> 'Ante mare et terras et quod tegit omnia cœlum,
> Unus erat toto naturæ vultus in orbe,
> Quem dixêre Chaos, rudis indigestaque moles,
> Nec quicquam nisi pondus iners, congestaque eodem
> Non bene junctarum discordia semina rerum.
> Nullus adhuc mundo præbebat lumina Titan,
> Nec nova crescendo reparabat cornua Phœbe,
> Nec circumfuso pendebat in aëre tellus,
> Ponderibus librata suis, nec brachia longo
> Margine terrarum porrexerat Amphitrite.
> Quâque erat et tellus, illic et pontus et aër.
> Sic erat instabilis tellus, innabilis unda,
> Lucis egens aër.   Nulli sua forma manebat.'

If it be asked what we suppose to have been the primary form of the nebula (for although the earth was 'without form,' we are not told that the general mass was so), we may reply that there is no reason to believe that it had at first any *regular* form,

---

[1] His *Metamorphoses*, in fact, absurd as many of the stories are, were intended for a universal ancient history, although with the real events usually disguised, and, we may say, for a Bible of his own; for the even prays, though in heathen fashion, for divine inspiration.

> 'In nova fert animus mutatas dicere formas
> Corpora.   Dî coeptis (nam vos mutastis et illas)
> Aspirate meis; primâque ab origine mundi
> Ad mea perpetuum deducite tempora carmen.'

although that is immaterial to the hypothesis ; for any projecting portions would gradually fall in towards the general mass, and it would in the course of time assume a form very nearly spherical. Then, steadily though slowly [1] contracting, from the mutual attraction of its component molecules, all drawing and moving towards the common centre of gravity, but contracting least in its equatorial regions, in consequence of the force of gravity being partly counteracted by the centrifugal force arising from its rotation, it would assume the form of an oblate spheroid,—the same form which our own terraqueous globe has acquired from the same cause, but becoming more and more oblate as the contraction advanced, and the centrifugal force increased.

Resuming the narrative of the Bible ;—as to the subsequent clause, ' The Spirit of God moved upon the face of the waters,' there is the same vague idea in the minds of readers generally regarding the last word as there is regarding 'the deep' in the previous clause. We cannot, however, understand by the word *waters*, seas, oceans, or great lakes ; for, as we see from a subsequent verse, the time was

[1] Slowly indeed ! for if the nebula extended only to twice the width of Neptune's orbit, the force of gravity at the exterior would be little more than the 500,000th part of its force at the surface of the Earth now; so that the exterior zone would contract only the 2500th part of an inch in radius in the first second.

not yet come for collecting the waters into one place, and separating them from the dry land.[1] We are therefore compelled to seek for some other meaning to the word; and probably there was no word in the Hebrew language which could express more accurately than *water* or *waters*, the cloud of floating atoms, already, as we shall see immediately, becoming a gaseous or fluid mass. The *deep* was probably the immense space, and the *waters* were the light and flowing substance which filled that space. The two words harmonize.

'The Spirit of God' is usually understood to signify *the Holy Spirit*, who is thus represented as presiding over the work of creation, and ready afterwards to impart life to the vegetable and animal kingdoms. Some, however, have suggested that the expression 'of God' may mean merely *emanating from God*, or *created by Him*, as it does in some passages of the Bible;[2] or it may signify *great, mighty, irresistible*, as it does in other passages.[3]

[1] The idea of a 'universal ocean,' entertained by many, would no doubt give a different sense to the words *deep* and *waters*; but then how could the earth, covered by a uniform ocean, with a perfectly spheroidal surface, be said to be 'without form,' since it would have had a more regular form than it has ever had subsequently? Or if the Hebrew word *tohu* mean *confusion*, as some interpreters have it, where was the confusion in a smooth, ubiquitous ocean? Ovid certainly did not so understand the sense, when he said:

'Quâque erat et tellus, illic et pontus et aër.'

[2] As in Job i. 16, where we read of 'the fire of God.'

[3] Thus the marginal reading of the passage just quoted is *a great*

Then, since the word *spirit*, in Hebrew *ruach*, like the corresponding Greek word πνεῦμα, frequently denotes nothing more than *breath* or *wind*,[1] the expression 'Spirit of God' may possibly signify nothing more than the *wind of God*, or a *powerful wind*; and if so, it would be no forced interpretation to understand it as the grand rotatory motion originally imparted to the whole nebula,—a motion which would be greatest on the surface, in consequence of the falling in of the projecting portions of the nebula, supposing it not to have been of a form truly spheroidal on its first formation, but irregular. That motion would be worthy of especial notice, since from it, as we shall soon see, results so wonderful were to follow in the construction of the solar system. There is some support to this opinion in the fact that the work of the first two days of creation at least was a purely material, and not a spiritual work ; and our Saviour says: 'That which is born of the Spirit is spirit.'[2] It was not even a life-giving work. It may be that the expression is used in a double sense, referring both to the Holy Spirit as directing the great work, and to the material movement employed by him as his grand

fire; and when we read in Ps. xxxvi. of 'the great mountains,' we are told that the Hebrew words mean literally *the mountains of God;* and similarly in other passages.

[1] See Amos iv. 13.   [2] John iii. 6.

instrument in carrying it on ; thus standing for both
the type and the antitype.

'And God said, Let there be light: and there was light. And God
saw the light, that it was good: and God divided the light from the
darkness.'—GEN. I. 3, 4.

Our great nebula, which we supposed to be
originally dark and cold, would, from the mutual
attraction of its component molecules, undergo, as
has been said before, slow but advancing condensation ; and that would elicit the latent heat which it
contained,[1] rendering that heat sensible, and continually raising the temperature of the cloudy mass.[2]
When that was raised to a little above 700 degrees
in any part of the cloud, that part would attain a
faint degree of luminosity, increasing as the temperature rose, till the whole zone, or rather shell, in
which a sufficiently high temperature was attained,
would be lighted up with a blaze of splendour.
Then truly would be realized that glorious display

[1] The use of the expression *latent heat* commits us to no particular
theory regarding its nature. The old idea was, that heat is a substance; but the philosophy of the present day regards it rather as
some kind of motion excited among the atoms of the heated matter,
or in the ether filling their interstices. On the latter understanding,
the latent heat of any substance means nothing more than its capability of producing sensible heat from condensation, congelation,
liquefaction of vapour, or chemical change.

[2] For an attempted computation of the extraordinary intensity of
heat which would be excited in this way, and for other remarks on
the subject, see Note A, at the end of the volume.

described in so few and simple words: 'God said, Let there be light: and there was light.'

In that early stage of the world's history in which the book of Genesis was written, when science was yet in its infancy, could any words have been devised which could more happily express the first appearance of luminosity in God's creation? If it had been said that God *created* the light, it would have been almost [1] a decision that light is a material substance, and so would have cut short our investigations on the subject, and would have put a veto upon the opinion now generally held, that light is not a substance at all, but consists in the undulations of ether. It is merely said, 'Let there be light;' and if light be a substance, still there is no light, in the ordinary sense of the word, till the substance attain that velocity of emission, and that rapidity of vibratory movement, which render it truly luminous: so that, if light existed previously, it would be in a latent and not in an apparent state; or if light, in itself immaterial, consist of vibrations of an ethereal medium, then certainly there would be no light until the ether vibrated. In either case, the previous state of the nebula would be that of darkness.

[1] Not altogether; for it is said in Isa. xlv. 7, 'I form the light, and create darkness;' but the first and formal enunciation of the fact is given in language as it were more guarded.

Again, could any expression be more majestic in
its very simplicity ? Considering what light is, as
we now know it,—considering its astonishing velocity
of 198,000 miles per second,—its diffusion through
space in every direction, from all luminous or
illuminated bodies, at the same instant, without
confusion or collisions,— its power of producing
distinct vision in the human eye, although falling
on it in an apparent chaos of rays, or waves, from
every visible point at once, and giving distinct information regarding the numbers, forms, motions,
colours, of multitudes of objects, at all distances and
in all directions,—its laws of reflection and refraction,—its separation by refraction into rays of different colours, to say nothing of the calorific and
actinic rays, and its further separation by the same
means into thousands of rays of different and defi-
nite degrees of refrangibility, giving rise to the
multitude of dark lines in the solar spectrum,—the
change by reflection in its mode of vibration, constituting what is called its *polarization*, attended by
all the beautiful phenomena involved in that word,
—and, finally, its inconceivably rapid rate of vibration, up to hundreds of millions of millions [1] of undulations every second ;—considering all this, could
anything have been more marvellous than its sudden

---

[1] The repetition of the word is not a typographical error.

appearance in chaos, at the sublimely authoritative command—*Let there be light?*

Considering also its indispensable utility, not only to the human eye, but to the whole vegetable and animal creation which was afterwards to come into existence, well may it be added—*God saw the light, that it was good.*

'God divided the light from the darkness.' On our hypothesis, this must have occurred; for the degree of luminosity would be very different in different parts of the nebula, and the non-luminous portions would be utterly impervious to the light which radiated from the other parts. Theoretical considerations show us that *the light could not have broken forth simultaneously in all parts of the nebula,* —that the maximum of heat and of light could scarcely be in the centre of the spheroidal cloud,— that it might be on its surface; but more probably was in some shell intermediate between the two,— and also that both the light and the heat would be greater in the polar than in the equatorial regions.[1]

From the higher temperature a part of the solid molecules (a small part at first) would become a gaseous atmosphere, in which the remainder would for a time float, rendering it a very bad medium for the transmission of light. The stratum or shell,

[1] For the reasons on which these conclusions are founded, see Note D.

therefore, which was first lighted up would not illuminate the others by radiation ; for the thick mist
would intercept the rays, and *that* to such an extent
that at a very short distance from any luminous part
of the nebula there would be total darkness.   No
doubt there would be a gradual shading off from a
stratum of glowing splendour to others of lower and
lower intensity of light; but as soon as a temperature of seven or eight hundred degrees was reached
on either side, all beyond would be darkness,—with
no luminosity in itself, and unrelieved by a single
ray of radiated light.   There would be *absolute
separation* between light and darkness. Truly
might it be said—*God divided the light from the
darkness.*

Now, before going further, let us give our attention to the marvellous character of this singular
expression.   What writer describing anything but a
reality such as we have just been contemplating,
would ever have thought of using such a form of
words?   Who would have thought it necessary to
mention the separation of conditions so opposed to
each other as those of light and darkness, or could
have imagined any method by which, before the
appearance of the solar orb, with its rays intercepted
by an opaque earth, light could have been separated
from darkness, unless in some way either insignificant or unintelligible?   For if our world had then

existed as a globe illuminated on its own surface, as seems to be the usual idea, it would only have been natural to suppose that its light would have radiated all around, and lighted up the solar system more or less, so that it could not have been said that the light was divided from the darkness. What uninspired writer, at all events, could have imagined the peculiar and grand way in which Laplace's wonderful hypothesis, when followed out to its necessary consequences, shows us that the separation must have been effected, if that hypothesis is a true one, as it appears to be,—or *any* such peculiar way as would have rendered the fact of the separation worth mentioning? Neither, as said before, can any one fancy that Laplace devised his hypothesis with any view of elucidating or defending the inspired records. Ovid's happy imagination has not dared to venture on this ground.

In giving attention thus far to the effects of condensation, nothing has been said regarding those which might have arisen from chemical action; for if the atoms of matter, as originally created, were simple, then a very large part of them would consist of the inflammable bases of metals, including hydrogen, then in a solid form, while another part, constituting perhaps all the remainder, would be oxygen, and other supporters of combustion. But when we consider that the nebula must have originally ex-

tended beyond the orbit of Neptune, and must consequently have been at least two hundred million
times less dense than our atmosphere, and that,
from the extreme cold, all the atoms were in a
solid condition, and consequently so remote from
each other as to be entirely out of reach of chemical
attraction, we can easily see that it would be a long
time before any chemical combination would take
place. Even when the temperature rose to such a
degree as to permit the combination of the metallic
bases with oxygen, that effect would commence first
in those strata which were already in the course of
being illuminated by condensation, and the light
and heat arising from their combustion would no
more spread into contiguous strata than the light
and heat given out by condensation ; for they would
in themselves be unaccompanied by flame, and incapable of spreading unless by radiation. As to
hydrogen, it would require a very high temperature
in the contiguous solid matter before it could be
ignited from contact with that matter, even if the
hydrogen were unmixed, and still more when mixed
with uninflammable gases.[1] Ultimately, however,
the metallic bases would almost all combine with
oxygen ; and hydrogen, first passing from the solid
to the gaseous state, would kindle into flame, pro-

[1] We know, for instance, that hydrogen gas is not combustible
when mixed with muriatic (or hydrochloric) acid.

bably lighting up the close of the first day with a grand conflagration, resulting in the production of an immense cloud of watery vapour. But that flame would not at once spread through the whole of the nebula,[1] being limited externally and internally by the extent of the gaseous shell, and being much checked in the rapidity of its progress by the very vapour which it had produced.

'And God called the light Day, and the darkness he called Night. And the evening and the morning were the first day.'—GEN. I. 5.

It is evident that the word *day*, in the latter clause of this verse, has not the same meaning as the same word in the first clause; for in the first it is distinguished from the night, whereas in the second it includes it. There is the same double use of the word *day* in ordinary language. It seems

[1] We know, indeed, from recent observations, that it did not do so, and that much of the hydrogen then remained and still remains unconsumed; for spectrum analysis detects its presence in the flames which still issue from the body of the sun. The centre of the sun becoming, as shown in Note B, the coldest region in the nebula, is probably still cold enough to retain hydrogen in a solid condition; and *that*, as the external heat reaches it, becomes aëriform, passes outward till it reaches the surface, and there kindles, still continuing the process which, according to our view, proceeded on a more extensive scale at the close of the first day. There are, however, it is undeniable, some difficulties attending this part of our subject,—that is, in regard to chemical considerations; but it is not reasonable to expect that a subject so recondite should be cleared altogether of difficulties in our still imperfect state of knowledge. It is not from too much science that our difficulties arise, but from too little.

also perfectly clear from the text itself, that the
day of the latter clause could not be a solar day of
twenty-four hours, and could not be intended as such
by the author of Genesis, even if he had been uninspired, since there was then, according to his own
words, no ' sun to rule the day,' while, according to
our hypothesis, there was not even a rotating earth
to measure out the hours.   The *day*, in all probability, meant some very long period of time ; and
since an evening and a morning are mentioned in
it, it may have meant that period which comprehended the transition from total darkness to the
universal diffusion of light over the whole surface of
the great spheroid, and even through its whole substance,—all except, probably, the central mass.

CHAPTER II.

THE SECOND DAY.

'And God said, Let there be a firmament in the midst of the waters, and let it divide the waters from the waters. And God made the firmament, and divided the waters which were under the firmament from the waters which were above the firmament : and it was so.'— GEN. I. 6, 7.

WHILE the darkness of the chaotic mass was gradually giving place to light, it must not be understood that no other change was going on ; for the light itself, we have seen, was mainly the result of condensation, and that condensation would give rise to a more and more oblate form of the spheroidal mass, as said above ; for, as the nebulous matter drew nearer towards the centre, it would bring with it the same absolute velocity which it had previously,—that is, the velocity of rotation ; and that, with a shorter radius, would give a greater angular velocity round the centre, and an increased centrifugal force.

If ultimately the centrifugal force of the external zone at the equator became so great as to be equal to the centripetal force, the matter of that zone would cease to approach towards the centre, and

would remain in perpetual revolution at a constant
distance from it ; whereas all within that zone, having
a smaller centrifugal and a greater centripetal force,
would continue to be drawn in, and would leave the
outer zone in the form of a ring.[1]

But if we had no other augmentation of the
centrifugal force than that which results from the
transference of the rotatory motion from a larger
radius to a smaller, that force would increase no
faster than in the inverse ratio of the distance, and
would consequently never become equal to the
centripetal force, which increases in the same proportion as *the square* of the distance diminishes.
But, as is well known, in the movements of the
planets an additional impetus is given to the moving molecule, as it approaches the centre of attraction, by the centripetal force itself ; and this, united

[1] 'Le point où la force centrifuge balance la pesanteur, est d'autant
plus près du corps, que le mouvement de rotation est plus rapide.
En concevant que l'atmosphère s'étende jusqu'à cette limite, et qu'en-
suite elle se resserre et se condense par le refroidissement à la surface
du corps, le mouvement de rotation deviendra de plus en plus rapide,
et la plus grande limite de l'atmosphère se rapprochera sans cesse de
son centre.   L'atmosphère abandonnera donc successivement, dans le
plan de son équateur, des zones fluides qui continueront de circuler
autour du corps, puisque leur force centrifuge est égale a leur pesanteur ; mais cette égalité n'ayant point lieu relativement aux molécules
de l'atmosphère éloignées de l'équateur, elles ne cesseront point de lui
appartenir.'—*Système du Monde,* liv. iv. ch. x.   Laplace's attributing the condensation to cooling, which I have ventured to assign to
centripetal force, does not at all affect the mechanical results.   The
atmosphere he speaks of is, of course, the substance of the nebula.

with the original movement in rotation, augments
so much the centrifugal force, that it ultimately
becomes equal to the centripetal, and would exceed
it if its movement inward were continued. This
will be evident from the consideration that, if there
were only one molecule, it would move round the
centre of attraction in an elliptic orbit, with its
centrifugal force continually increasing as it drew
nearer the centre, until at its perihelion [1] that force
would become so much greater than the centripetal,
as to carry the molecule back to its original distance.
Then if, instead of a single molecule, there were a
countless number, all drawn in towards the centre,
their mutual perturbations would not affect the total
motion in rotation or the centrifugal force. But
these perturbations, especially when the solid molecules came to be surrounded by a gaseous atmosphere, would have the effect of uniting them all
into one body,[2] revolving collectively at the mean
distance,—namely, that at which the two forces
would be balanced,—instead of continuing in a dance
of independent orbits between the extreme distances.

After the first ring was thrown off, the remainder

[1] That is, supposing the attracting mass to be wholly within its
orbit, and constant ; but in the case before us, if that were not so,
the slight difference would not be worth consideration.

[2] Not, of course, a solid body, but one connected system or
nebulous mass.

D

of the nebula would continue to contract, throwing off another and another ring in succession, with no termination to the process, until the central mass refused to contract further, in consequence of the attainment of a liquid or of a solid condition.

The formation of one of the inner rings might possibly commence before that of the outermost ring would be completed. As far as our subject is concerned, however, that is a point of no consequence, provided that a certain number of rings were ultimately formed in this way; and assuredly they would be so formed if we start with the conditions supposed.[1]

Each ring, its substance having previously been greatly heated by the condensation of the nebula, but being now more freely exposed, would slowly cool by radiation into external space, and the ring would be contracted in its sectional area; but the distance of the centre of gravity of that section from the centre of the nebula would remain unchanged, and would henceforth become a fixed quantity, the centrifugal force caused by its revolution round the general centre remaining, as at its first separation,

[1] A very pretty mechanical illustration is sometimes exhibited of the formation of rings by centrifugal force, effected by the rapid rotation of a basin of watery liquid, in the centre of which a globe of oil is placed of the same specific gravity. This can be accepted, however, only as a popular illustration, since laws and circumstances entirely differ in the two cases.

exactly equal to its attraction towards it. The length of the ring,[1] if we may so express it, would remain constant, while its sectional area would contract more and more, till at last, like any other fluid cylinder when reduced in width below a certain proportion to its length, its internal equilibrium would become instable, and it would be ready to break at one or more places as soon as the slightest irregularity arose in any one part ; and unless the nebula had been a perfect sphere at the outset, irregularities would arise from the falling in of the projecting portions, and these irregularities would never be altogether obliterated so long as the nebula remained in a fluid state. The breaking of a liquid cylinder into separate fragments, when it becomes too much elongated, we may see exemplified by drawing out a thread of half-melted wax, and then exposing it to a greater heat, when it runs at once into drops ; or by sending through a fine iron wire, stretched horizontally over a table, a current of electricity sufficiently strong to melt the wire : when so melted, it does not fall on the table as a continuous thread, but in separate drops. A ring, it will be observed, is only a cylinder bent round.

If the nebulous ring were not very much elongated, relatively to its thickness, it would break at

---

[1] That is, the circumference passing through the centres of gravity of the various sections.

only one point. If otherwise, it might break at more points than one. But however divided, the broken ring, or each portion of it, would rapidly draw in its extremities and collect itself into a globular mass, revolving round the great central nebula with the same velocity with which the ring itself previously revolved.

Before going further, let us consider what would occur to such a mass, so revolving, at first always keeping the same side towards the general centre, exactly as the ring itself did, and at the same time contracting in volume. Such a globe, although it might be regarded on first thoughts as not rotating, would really have a rotation on its own axis, with its period of rotation exactly equal to that of its revolution, as in the case of our moon; and *that*, so far from being merely an imaginary or nominal rotation, would have all the physical effects of any other actual rotation, bringing the globe, still nebulous, into a form oblately spheroidal at first, and, on subsequent contraction, causing it to become more and more oblate, for the same reasons as those already given in the case of the great nebula.[1] For similar

[1] This, to those who have a difficulty in understanding how a motion like that of the moon can involve rotation as well as revolution, might be explained in another way; namely, by showing how the matter on the outer side of the newly-formed globe, having a greater velocity, and that on the inner side having a smaller velocity, than the centre of the globe, would both tend, when drawn nearer the said

reasons, an expansion of the globe would retard the rotation, although it would never wholly destroy it.

Now when a ring, or any considerable part of a ring, suddenly collapsed into a globe, the first effect would be an expansion of the diameter of the globe as more and more matter fell into it, and consequently a retardation of the rotatory movement which it would have had but for such an expansion, giving an appearance, as seen from the centre of the nebula, of a retrograde rotation. But subsequent contraction, from gravitation towards its own centre, and from loss of heat by radiation, would again quicken the rotation; and ultimately that might be so much accelerated, and the oblateness of the spheroid so much increased,[1] that one or more rings might be thrown off from it, in the same manner as in the case of the principal nebula.

We have now, then, arrived at that period in which the primary planets—most of them at least—have come into existence, but still merely as spheroidal masses of vapour, with solid molecules perhaps floating in the vapour, all the exterior beyond Mars, and also the earth, being encompassed by one

centre, to produce a direct rotation, and to increase it when already produced.

[1] It would thus appear that the ultimate rapidity of rotation of any planet depends on the extent to which its equatorial diameter is less than the width of the ring from which it was formed,—a consideration which might lead to some curious computations. —See Note C.

or more rings, and some of them perhaps having attained a still more advanced stage.

As soon as the spheroidal cloud, the material of the future earth, was separated from the nebulous ring which surrounded it, a great expanse began to be interposed, separating by an impassable gulf everything on the earth beneath, or on that which was to be the earth, from everything in the heavens above. That expanse is probably what was meant by the *firmament*—not limited, however, by the orbit of our satellite, but stretching out into the whole extent of space.

The English word *firmament* has been unhappily chosen as the rendering of the word *rakiah*, improperly suggesting to the unlearned reader the idea of firmness or solidity. In the original Hebrew, however, the word, we are told, conveys nothing of the idea of firmness, or of a material character of any kind, but simply of expansion or extent,[1] and is alike applicable to a vacuum and to a space occupied by aëriform matter. In other parts of the Scriptures it is used sometimes for our own atmosphere, sometimes for the great expanse in which the stars are placed. Giving, then, to the word *waters* the same interpretation which we were compelled to assign to it in the second verse—that is, the mass of the nebula now in a gaseous state, but gradually

[1] See Note D.

passing into that of liquidity—we appear to be informed in the seventh verse, interpreting it by means of Laplace's hypothesis, that the Almighty now cut off from the mass of the nebula that portion of it which was afterwards to become our terraqueous globe, and separated it from the remainder by a great vacant or ethereal space.

There is another view of what *might* be meant by the 'waters above the firmament,' and that not at all an improbable one. At the period which we have now reached, in consequence of the high temperature of the earth, all the waters of its rivers, lakes, seas, and oceans, could exist only in the state of steam. Considering the enormous space that steam occupies comparatively with water,—the still greater extent to which it expands when more highly heated, and the extreme rarefaction which would exist in the upper regions of such an atmosphere, not only from the absence of pressure, but from the extremely low force of gravity at very great distances from the centre,—considering also that room was required for a great variety of other gaseous matter still uncondensed;—considering all this, we should probably not be rash if we assumed that the great cloud of steam then surrounding our globe extended at that period nearly as far as the moon's orbit, and that, in contracting, the upper shell of it acquired sufficient centrifugal force to

retain it at a high elevation,—in the form, in short,
of a second or inner ring revolving round the earth.
Then, when the cooling process advanced further,
it would be a ring of water, or of separate watery
drops. These might be *the waters above the firmament.* In fact, it is not easy to see how the formation of such a ring could be avoided at first, although
it is easy to see how it might not be permanent. It
is not at all improbable, indeed, that besides a ring
of water, there were rings of other substances, which,
dropping successively to the earth's surface at different epochs, gave a distinct mineral character to the
geological systems of rocks which were under the
course of formation at the different periods.[1]

Before leaving the subject of rings, for the present at least, I delay a little to answer a question
which is likely to occur to many to whom astronomical studies are not familiar. Have we anything,
tangible or visible, still existing, on which we can
support our hypothesis of nebulæ and of rings?
Undoubtedly we have. Looking to the starry sky
with a good telescope, we observe nebulæ, as Sir
William Herschel first pointed out, apparently in
all stages of their growth—pure nebulæ—nebulous
rings — nebulous clusters — nebulous stars — and

---

[1] How otherwise, for instance, can we explain the fact that no
strata but those which consisted almost wholly of lime, or carbonate
of lime, were deposited in the latter part of the cretaceous period?

clearly-defined or fully-formed stars; and although
some of those which Sir William and others regarded as mere clouds of 'star dust' or vapour, such
as we have supposed our system to have commenced with, have since been resolved by telescopes
of higher power into numerous separate stars, yet
there are others which never have been so resolved;
and more recent spectrum-observations appear to
have established as a fact, that some of them are
really gaseous, or partly gaseous, clouds, and have
even detected the existence of gaseous matter of
various kinds in the atmosphere of our own sun.[1]

Again, around the planet Saturn we have several
rings, similar to those described as the natural consequences of our hypothesis, still revolving in great
beauty, unbroken into satellites, and puzzling our
astronomers by the stability of their equilibrium,
as if they had been preserved till the period of
man's existence, as specimens of the great scheme
by which the solar system was formed. Yet more,
we have the remains of a nebulous ring, still revolving unabsorbed round our own sun, although never
wholly separated from it, and visible to us, as the
zodiacal light, when the Earth comes in her annual
orbit into such a position that we can see it not across
its thin body, but along its greater dimensions,—not

[1] For some further observations on this part of our subject, see
Note E.

sideways, but edgeways,—in the same position, in
short, in which a spectator observes the shadow of a
steeple become visible in a mist, appearing as a dark
column above it, while it is invisible from every
other direction. It is a ring *in embryo*, as it were,
like the inner transparent ring of Saturn. And,
finally, we have an irregular ring of meteoric bodies
revolving round the Sun in a singularly eccentric
orbit,[1] extending, it is believed, from the orbit of
the Earth to that of Neptune, and becoming visible
occasionally to us, as *the November shower*, when the
Earth passes through it, kindling up its separate
bodies by collision with our atmosphere.

'And God called the firmament Heaven. And the evening and
the morning were the second day.'—GEN. I. 8.

The firmament, as we have seen, may have been
our atmosphere, but at that time immeasurably
greater in volume than it is now, not only from expansion by heat, but from containing, in the form of
steam, all the waters of our present seas, lakes, and
rivers, and several other more or less volatile elements besides, and from its extreme rarity in the
higher regions. It is more probable, however, that
the name included, besides our grosser atmosphere,
that more ethereal medium which is now generally

[1] Or, as some think, in an orbit nearly circular, at about the same
distance as the Earth from the Sun.

believed to fill all space, as far at least as the utmost bounds of the starry universe. In accordance with this view, the word *heaven* or *heavens*, here identified with *firmament*, is used in various passages of the sacred Scriptures, at one time for the lower atmosphere in which the, birds fly, and at another time for the greater expanse in which the planets revolve and the fixed stars shine. The corresponding words in Greek, Latin, and English, οὐρανός, *cælum*, *heaven* or *heavens*, have the same latitude, and are also extended, like the Hebrew word for heaven, beyond the material creation to the abode of God (or 'of the gods') and of the angels.

What were *the evening and the morning* of the second day, it is not easy to see. Apparently they were not a literal evening and morning, even with the extension to a lengthened period of time, for the day did not begin in material darkness and end in material light. But it began with the earth and the heavens in a condition of apparently hopeless conflagration, evening enough to the limited understandings even of angels, and it ends with a morning of hope in the appearance of a round earth at last, or at least its nucleus, already revolving in its annual orbit, and rotating on its axis, and of several of the other planets, if not the whole, in the same condition. It was the morning of a new state of things.

CHAPTER III.

THE THIRD DAY.

'And God said, Let the waters under the heaven be gathered together into one place, and let the dry land appear: and it was so.
And God called the dry land Earth; and the gathering together of
the waters called he Seas: and God saw that it was good.'—GEN. L
9, 10.

CONSIDERING the extreme brevity of our
narrative, compared with the inconceivably
long periods over which the events related extend,
it is not to be wondered at that the steps of the
former are short relatively to the latter, and that a
single step passes over vast and numerous changes.
This will be peculiarly conspicuous in the events of
the third day.

At the close of the second day we left the Earth
a mere nucleus of melted matter surrounded by a
deep, dense, and impure atmosphere, and the Moon
still a ring of vapour, but also possibly with a
liquid nucleus running centrally round within it,[1] as
a cylindrical axis.

[1] If we can conceive that the ring, the material of the future Moon,
had attained to a great extent the liquid condition before it broke
and drew together to form a globe, that would at once, from the principles established in page 53, account for the very slow rotation of the
Moon on its axis, which, although it might not at first be, as it is

That ring, however, now on the third day, parts
in two, and runs together into a spherical cloud
with a liquid centre; while the Earth, after collecting
all of its less volatile vapour into its molten orb,
cooling still further, begins to form a crust over its
surface, like ice over a lake. Now, however, the
temperature has sunk so low that the atmosphere
is no longer luminous; but everywhere over the
boundless plain volcanic craters rise, lighting up the
gloomy expanse with their ghastly fires, and toss-
ing out torrents of lava, mud, and ashes, into the
already dense atmosphere.[1] The watery vapour now
begins to be condensed, falling in heavy showers,
washing down with it the mud and ashes of the
volcanoes, and the grosser ingredients yet floating
in the atmosphere, and thus depositing over the
solidified crust stratum upon stratum of soft material, afterwards to be dried and hardened by the

now, *exactly* coincident in time with its revolution round the Earth,
would ultimately come into *perfect* agreement with it, provided that
it had an *approximate* coincidence to begin with, and provided that
the Moon remained some time in a fluid condition. Laplace, however,
proceeds as if such an original approximation were unnecessary; but
it would certainly facilitate the ultimate adjustment; and whatever
view we take of that, the ultimate adjustment itself is unexplainable
unless on the hypothesis of an originally fluid condition of the Moon.

[1] The description here given is not hypothetical, for the state of
things which then prevailed has not yet altogether ended, and a
similar scene, on a very reduced scale, may still be seen. For a
description of it, see Note F. The present condition of the Silurian
and older rocks also testify, to a certain extent, to its reality.

heat below. No mountain chains of any considerable height as yet obstruct or turn aside the winds,
so that they blow with fury, and for long periods of
time, unvaried in direction, ruffling the tenacious
surface, driving along volcanic or meteoric sand and
ashes, and dashing them with fury on the successive
muddy strata.[1] The showers of rain, as they fall,
rapidly evaporate, so that we have nowhere any
depth of water, and yet the ground is seldom dry.
This is proved by the rippled surfaces,[2] by the tracks
of annelides, if such they were, or if not by the
prints of the *palæocorda*, and of many other fucoid
and probably fungous plants, and by the impressions made by strong winds, as well as showers of
rain and of sand,[3]—and all these, where they are seen
at all, much the same on the surfaces of the lowest
strata as on those of the highest, with at least some
thousands of feet of thickness intervening.[4]

[1] This picture is not, any more than the preceding, fanciful, but is
derived from close observation of the older rocks, especially the Lower
Silurian. Numerous specimens might be produced to prove all that
has been said.

[2] We are not *sure* that these ripples may not be formed under deep
water, but the other proofs are clear and decisive.

[3] The marks made by sand-showers are much more common, in the
Lower Silurian rocks which I have examined, than those made by rain,
probably from the latter being generally washed away as soon as they
were formed.

[4] And yet a writer, who professes to be wiser than Moses, speaking
of the Silurian rocks, says: 'These strata were deposited at the bottom
of the sea, and the remains are exclusively marine.'—*Essays and Reviews*, Mosaic Cosmogony, p. 214.

Contractions of the earth's bulk from cooling, or expansion of that portion of it which was changing from a liquid to a solid condition, or volcanic disturbances, or unequal loading of the crust, or more than one of these causes uniting their effects, at last bend and break the crust, turning up most of its masses on their sides, and forming rugged rocks standing out with their jagged edges from the midst of the ocean of molten rock now again uncovered. This process is repeated again and again at subsequent periods, and in its repetition are formed successively the rocks of the Laurentian, the Cambrian, and the Silurian systems,—the latter of these in part from the wasted materials of the former.

At the close of this period the surface is more cooled, rain lies longer upon it unevaporated, and now flows into the deep hollows made by the broken and uptilted masses of rock. As late as the time of the Lower Silurian formation, it has usually been said that no plants existed except some fucoids; and along with these, a few zoophytes, small crustaceans, and molluscs.[1] And if a greater variety of plants have

---

[1] 'The Laurentian rocks of North America, Britain, Bavaria, Bohemia, and possibly of Scandinavia, forming the foundations on which all the other strata have been accumulated, were characterized,' in the preceding part of the volume, 'as containing specimens of the lowest grade of animal life, in the shape of a marine foraminifer, the eozoon. It was then pointed out that the next succeeding deposits, or those of

recently been found in the Lower Silurian strata,
they appear to have been either fucoids growing in
brackish pools, or fungi, mosses, and other plants
hastily springing up on their moist banks, and soon
covered over by fresh deluges of mud, while the
molluscs and crustaceans could scarcely find pools
deep enough to cover them, the latter leaving still
visible the scratches made by their feet as they
attempted to swim in the shallow water;[1] but by

the Cambrian age, though of enormous dimensions, and often but
slightly altered mud and sand, contained only the rarest trace of anything higher in organization than a zoophyte. Next it was shown
that the following or Silurian formations exhibited, even in their very
bottom beds, a considerable augmentation of animal life, as shown by
the presence of crustaceans, molluscs, and zoophytes, occupying layers
at similar horizons in the crust of the earth in very distant regions.
Proceeding upwards from the earliest of these zones, we then ascended
to other sediments, in which we recognised a more copious distribution
of marine creatures, closely resembling each other, though imbedded
in rocks separated by wide seas, and now often raised up into the
loftiest mountains. Examining all the strata exposed to view that
were formed during the first long natural epoch of the life which I
termed 'Silurian,' we found that the successive deposits were charged
with a great variety of forms, such as the trilobite or primeval
crustacean, with a few of the earliest chambered shells, as well as
numerous exquisitely formed molluscs, crinoids, and zoophytes—the
families of Cystideans and Graptolites being exclusively found in these
Silurian rocks.'—*Siluria*, by Sir Roderick I. Murchison, fourth
edition, ch. xx. p. 476.

Mountains, higher than they are now, probably existed at the close
of the Silurian period, but none whatever at the commencement of
the Laurentian.

[1] Sir Roderick Murchison, no doubt, sometimes speaks of extensive
and deep seas in the older periods, but as a mere assumption, with no
corroborative facts in support of it.

the time that the Upper Silurian rocks are deposited, the crustaceans become of larger species,[1] while numbers of floating shells, particularly *Orthocerata,*[2] now indicate the presence of water deep enough for them to swim or to float in ; and just before the close of the Silurian period, a few solitary fishes appear for the first time, having at last found seas in which their evolutions and locomotions would be unfettered. *The waters begin to be gathered into one place;* and, as if to enable us to finish our sentence in the words of the Bible, at that very epoch, geologists testify,[3] for the first time since creation began, traces of true dry-land plants are seen,[4] for *the dry land had begun to appear.* Could any written record be more clearly established and illustrated than that of our text is by the recently dug up tablets of stone ? It is almost as if it were written at the end of the verse in plain language,—'For this is the close of the

<hr>

[1] As the *Pterygotus* and the *Eurypterus.*

[2] *Siluria*, ch. xx. p. 486.

[3] 'On the same occasion we observed that the only remains of small land plants (one of which seemed to be a stem, and the others numerous seeds, termed "spore-cases of Lycopodiaceæ" by Dr. Hooker) occurred in beds above the uppermost fish layer, and therefore at the very top of the Ludlow formation, just beneath the lowest beds of the Old Red.'—*Siluria*, ch. x. p. 241, footnote. See also the same work, ch. vii. p. 138.

[4] If any of the plants whose impressions have more recently been found in the Lower Silurian rocks should prove to be true dry-land plants, we have merely to transfer the epoch of the separation of land and sea from the close to the beginning of the Silurian age.

E

Silurian age;' and as if it were inscribed on the
Silurian strata—'These were deposited on the third
day of creation.'

But we are not yet come to that which was properly the age of fishes.[1]   As yet they are few and of
only one order, the *Ganoid*, and these armed with
coats of mail, in order probably to enable them to
withstand the high temperature[2] or its rapid changes,
or perhaps to guard them against dangerous com-
motions among stormy waters.

Of the crustaceans of the later Silurian periods, by
far the most abundant are of that peculiar class
called *Trilobites;* 'a family,' in the words of Hugh
Miller, 'in whose nicely jointed shells the armourer
of the middle ages might have found almost all the
contrivances of his art anticipated, with not a few
besides which he had failed to discover.'

Of these there is no more remarkable feature than
their large and beautifully constructed eyes.   Now
what would unbelievers have said regarding these if
the third verse of our chapter had by any means
been omitted ?   They would have exclaimed : 'Your

[1] 'The three or four peculiar fishes just enumerated may be viewed
as the heralds which announced the close of the Silurian era in Britain,
and the advent of the numerous other families of this class, which
thenceforward are found in all the younger sediments.'—*Siluria*, ch.
x. p. 242.

[2] Fishes similarly clothed are still found in the Red Sea, to the
high temperature of which there are now daily many unwilling
witnesses.

whole theory falls to the ground ; for here are creatures which had perfectly formed eyes long before
there was a sun, according to your own account, to
supply them with light.' But Geology and Genesis
agree in testifying that there was light even then,
and yet (as we shall see subsequently) that there was
no sun.

Following our history, as recorded in the rocks,
we now come to the *Devonian* system, or in other
words, the *Old Red Sandstone,* showing in the clearest
manner that the waters *have now been* gathered into
one place, and that the dry land *has already* appeared ;
for they consist of a succession of strata, not formed
among shallow pools of rain-water collected over
plains of sand and clay, but deposited from muddy
water washed down by impetuous rivers, and running
into seas worthy of the name,—seas peopled by
numerous fishes of various kinds, and these still
protected by strong defensive armour.[1] At the
same time, coniferous trees, calamites, and tree
ferns, washed down by the floods into the sea, to
be deposited in its bed, testify equally clearly to
the existence of dry land.

Again, we are told that 'God saw that it was good.'
No wonder that he did so ! Here was one of his
worlds, a world afterwards to be distinguished above

---

[1] For a full and interesting account of these, see Mr. Miller's *Old Red Sandstone.*

all others, formed in such a wondrous manner, out
of a mass at first dark, cold, chaotic, '*tohu and bohu,*'
confusion and emptiness, and afterwards kindled up
into a fearful conflagration, but now showing land
and sea, rivers and mountains, and exhibiting the
beginnings of vegetable and of animal life, the first
fruits of better things to come, which *he, and he
only*, could foresee.

'And God said, Let the earth bring forth grass, the herb yielding
seed, and the fruit-tree yielding fruit after his kind, whose seed is in
itself, upon the earth : and it was so. And the earth brought forth
grass, and herb yielding seed after his kind, and the tree yielding
fruit, whose seed was in itself, after his kind : and God saw that it
was good.'—GEN. I. II, 12.

Next after the *Devonian* we have the *Carboniferous* system of rocks. These are composed partly
of strata of lime and sand, again deposited from the
sea, and partly of great stratified accumulations of
trees and herbs, which at that period grew in rank
profusion, and afterwards, when prostrated and
pressed down by layers of marine deposits heaped
upon them, were in the course of time converted
into coal for the use of future inhabitants, thus provided for, although as yet known only to the fore-
sight of the Almighty.

There are two theories as to the way in which
our coal-fields were prepared, for the discussion of
which the reader is referred to any of our treatises

on the subject; but in whatever way the grand work was accomplished, one thing is certain, that at that period vegetable life sprung up in teeming profusion, as if the new and warm earth, not now too warm, delighted to pour it forth,—to such an extent, that nearly one thousand different species of plants then grew which the world had never seen before.[1]

No doubt we have no specimen of *grass* of that age corresponding to those which now cover our pasture grounds : but it is not said that it was the same as our grass ; and it is not likely to have been so, for there were then no grass-eating quadrupeds to browse upon it. 'The humblest grass in our meadows,' says Hugh Miller, when· discussing another subject, "belongs to the same natural order as the tall bamboo, that, shooting up its panicles amid the jungles of India to the height of sixty feet, looks down upon all the second-class trees of the country.' Probably, however, the word was used in ancient times in a still more general sense than even that. When our Saviour spoke of 'the grass which is to-day in the field, and to-morrow is cast into the oven,' he was not speaking of grass

[1] 'In the standard work of Bronn, von Meyer, and Göppert, which gives the most complete tabular view of ancient nature hitherto published, Professor Göppert estimates the total number of known species of fossil plants of this great Carboniferous era as 934.'— *Siluria*, ch. xii, p. 286.

at all, in our sense of the word, but of lilies. In fact, the one clause of the twelfth verse seems to explain the other ; for if, before *herb*, we omit the word *and*, which is not in the original, it reads: ' And the earth brought forth grass, herb yielding seed,' etc. Probably all that is meant by *grass* in this passage is simply *green herbage.*

Neither are we necessarily to understand by *fruit* such soft fruits as form luxurious food for man, although such might have been in abundance, without leaving any specimens of articles so perishable for our inspection. Among such multitudes of herbs and trees as then grew, and of so many varieties, fruits there must have been, but such fruits as were adapted to the consumption of animals then living, or simply receptacles for containing the seed and bringing it to maturity.

With these provisos, then, we may ask any observer of the rocks, which of all the geological periods he would fix upon as corresponding to the two verses last quoted, and he will say at once, the Carboniferous. ' It was emphatically,' says Mr. Miller,[1] 'the period of plants—"of herbs yielding seed after their kind." In no other age did the world ever witness such a flora : the youth of the earth was a peculiarly green and umbrageous youth,

[1] *The Testimony of the Rocks*, Lecture Third, p. 135 of first edition.

—a youth of dusk and tangled forests, of huge pines and stately araucarians, of the reed-like calamite, the tall tree-fern, the sculptured sigillaria, and the hirsute lepidodendron. Wherever dry land or shallow lake or running stream appeared, from where Melville Island now spreads out its icy wastes under the star of the pole, to where the arid plains of Australia lie solitary beneath the bright cross of the South, a rank and luxuriant *herbage* cumbered every foot-breadth of the dark and steaming soil. Of this extraordinary age of plants we have our cheerful remembrancers and witnesses, in the flames that roar in our chimneys when we pile up the winter fire ; in the brilliant gas which now casts its light on this great assemblage, and that lightens up the streets and lanes of this vast city (London) ; in the glowing furnaces that smelt our metals, and give moving power to our ponderous engines ; in the long dusky trains that, with shriek and snort, speed dart-like across our landscapes ; and in the great cloud-enveloped vessels that darken the lower reaches of your noble river, and rush in foam over ocean and sea. The geological evidence is so complete as to be patent to all, that the first great period of organized being was, as described by the Mosaic record, peculiarly a period of herbs and trees " yielding fruit after their kind." '

It will be observed, then, that we are now per-
using two contemporaneous histories,—one written
on papyrus or on parchment by Moses, the other
by the finger of God on tablets of rock,—the author
of the former knowing nothing whatever of the
records contained in the latter ; and on placing
the two together, as it were in parallel columns,
see how wonderfully they agree, not only now, but
in the previous stages, and in all that are to follow!
The reader will testify that not the slightest alteration is made here in the order of the verses, and
the geologist will also testify that no liberty is
taken with the order of sequence of the rocks.
Then let both observe how remarkably the two
histories correspond from step to step.   Doubtless the one is a mere abstract, requiring to be
written in a very narrow column, and with many
blank intervals, while the other is copiously filled
up in all its details, requiring a very wide column
of closely crowded writing ; but the coincidence is
not the less striking on that account.

Seeing the great beauty that the earth has now
assumed, and the immense utility of the stores
which it was this day accumulating for the future
use of a higher class of inhabitants, well might it
be repeated at the close of the Carboniferous era,
and still more manifestly than before : 'God saw
that it was good.'

'And the evening and the morning were the third day.'—GEN. I. 13.

We may take this either literally or figuratively :

Literally: there was an outward and visible change corresponding to the transition from night to day ; for the condensation of watery vapour shows us that, from the commencement of this period, the heat had so much diminished that the glowing splendour universally diffused during the previous day, had at the beginning of this wholly disappeared, and the still remaining impurity of the atmosphere confined the lights of the volcanoes to their own immediate centres, so that probably darkness generally prevailed ; but as the third day advances, the dense and impure fogs begin to be cleared away, and volcanic fires, gleaming in all directions, throw a light, though ghastly and lurid, over the whole face of the earth ; so that we have again passed from darkness to light.

Figuratively: there was again, during this day, the transition from a state of comparative hopelessness, as far as appearances went, to one of a most cheering kind. No doubt the termination of the previous day was hopeful compared with its commencement ; but it left the earth a mere nucleus of melted rock surrounded by a muddy atmosphere ; and the third day commences with no improvement on that, for even the light has disappeared. The slow dawning of brighter prospects, however, came,—in the transition from an outspread

barren plain to the same plain broken up and
diversified with ridges of rugged rocks; then to
a separation of land and sea,—a rough land, no
doubt, but showing a few patches of green vegetation at last, and a sea, tempestuous indeed, and
lashing the margin of a strangely wild, rocky, and
broken shore, yet with shoals of fishes enlivening
its waters; and, finally, to a landscape of lakes,
rivers, mountains, and diversified plains—the latter
covered with a more luxuriant vegetation than the
eye of man has ever beheld, and *that* not wasted,
but economically stored up for the use of some
future race, for whom the earth is now manifestly
being prepared, the very coals being prophetic.
In the beginning of the day there was a state of
things so gloomy, that even an angel would see
little ground for hope, and would 'walk by faith
and not by sight,' and *that* the more so since a
duration of time equivalent to hundreds of thousands, not to say millions, of our years probably
passed away during that gloomy evening before a
morning of brighter hope began to dawn.   For
the first time, perhaps, the faith of some wavered.
But at the close of the day, so bright would be the
prospect, that the heavenly hosts would be ready to
clap their wings with joy.   Order has at last sprung
out of chaos: κόσμος is κόσμος indeed. *The evening
and the morning were the third day.*

CHAPTER IV.

THE FOURTH DAY.

BEFORE entering upon the work of this day, let us inquire if any more direct proof can be given that the earth was really at one time in a condition so hot as I have described, in which the material of the rocks, on its surface at least, was actually melted. To answer this we may ask another question, namely : If the earth has at one time been so hot, in what condition would it be now ? It would be cooled on the outside, and retain more or less of its original heat within. And that is exactly the state in which we find it in our day.

As we descend below the surface of the earth in mines, we find that the temperature steadily increases. The rate of increase differs considerably in different places, owing to local peculiarities ; but the average, as far as has been ascertained hitherto, is about one degree of Fahrenheit for every fifty feet of descent, and *that* not falling off as the descent is continued. At a depth of seven or eight miles, therefore, everything must be red-hot, and at fifty miles down, the temperature must be more than five thousand degrees,—sufficient, probably, to melt every metal and every kind of rock [1] under ordinary circumstances,—that is, if they were relieved from the superincumbent pressure.[2] That pressure probably keeps them from fusion, and thus removes all the objections that have been raised against the theory of a high central heat ; but whatever effect the pressure may have in altering the melting point, it can have none whatever in keeping down the temperature. Suppose, then, the whole outer covering of the earth to be suddenly thrown off to the depth of fifty miles, we should find all within in the condition of a glowing molten mass, far hotter than any furnace which man has ever heated. It is in vain that any one sneers at the idea of the earth having *formerly* been in a state of intense heat, for it is so *even now*,[3]—all except a mere superficial coating, which could not but have cooled down to

[1] That I am not going beyond the usual estimate in this, will be seen from the following extract from Sir Charles Lyell's *Principles of Geology*, book ii. ch. xviii. : 'If we adopt M. Cordier's estimate, of 1° Fahr. for every 45 feet of depth, as the mean result, and assume, with the advocates of central fluidity, that the increasing temperature is continued downwards, we should reach the ordinary boiling point of water at about two miles below the surface, and at the depth of about twenty-four miles should arrive at the melting point of iron,—a heat sufficient to fuse almost every known substance.'

[2] For an explanation of this, and for some further remarks on the subject, see Note G.

[3] The case is exactly as if a visitor, walking through the outskirts

the state in which it now is, if it were allowed the time which geologists concur in demanding for the formation of their successive rock systems ; and that time is freely conceded to them.[1]

'And God said, Let there be lights in the firmament of the heaven, to divide the day from the night ; and let them be for signs, and for seasons, and for days, and for years : and let them be for lights in the firmament of the heaven, to give light upon the earth : and it was so. And God made two great lights ; the greater light to rule the day, and the lesser light to rule the night : the stars also. And God set them in the firmament of the heaven, to give light upon the earth, and to rule over the day and over the night, and to divide the light from the darkness : and God saw that it was good.'—GEN. I. 14-18.

During the third day, or even previously, all the nine primary rings of vapour had been formed, and probably also all the secondary ; all of the former and most of the latter having been broken up and consolidated into planets and satellites, and one of the primary rings having been divided, in consequence probably of its thinness, into more than a hundred separate parts. But there still remained

of an iron foundry, guided by one of the workmen, were to place his foot upon a heap of slag, and ask his conductor if he really means to assert that that cool heap was a short while before at a white heat, while the conductor replies by knocking off the top of it with his spade, and showing him that it is at a white heat still.

[1] 'Baron Fourier, after making a curious series of experiments on the cooling of incandescent bodies, has endeavoured, by profound mathematical calculations, to prove that the actual distribution of heat in the earth's envelope is precisely that which would have taken place if the globe had been formed in a medium of very high temperature, and had afterwards been constantly cooled.'—LYELL'S *Principles of Geology*, book i. ch. viii.

the great central cloud, now also cooling and condensing, but without acquiring sufficient centrifugal
force to throw off any additional rings. Great com-
pressive force would reduce it to a liquid, or, near
its centre, even to a solid condition, long before that
result could have been attained by the mere lower-
ing of its temperature. The purification of its
atmosphere would also be quickened by the great
force of gravity acting upon its grosser elements,
till at last, in the course of the fourth day, its
struggling rays make their way for the first time
into unlimited space,—it takes its place as a bright
star in the galaxy of the heavens, and it shines on
its attendant planets as a glorious orb, governing
their revolutions, and shedding down upon them
light and heat. Its beams for the first time fall on
the moon, and her waxing and waning crescents
throw them back to the earth, in testimony that
now the great Creator has no longer left the
terrestrial globe to be illuminated only by volcanic
fires, and to be warmed by an unvarying and
equally diffused central heat, with no alternation of
day and night, of summer and winter, but has at
last *placed lights in the heavens to divide the day from
the night, and to be for signs* (bi-monthly periods
perhaps) *and for seasons, and for days and for years,
—two great lights, the greater light to rule the day,
and the lesser light to rule the night.*

And the stars also; for they were likewise probably at first, similarly to our own solar system, mere nebulæ, created at the same time with it; and like it, they have, during the three preceding days, been gradually emerging into order, and at last shine forth, like our own sun, each probably attended by its own system of planets.[1]

No doubt the sun and the moon have been in the course of preparation in former days; but it is not until the fourth day that the work is completed. That which on the fourth day became the grand luminary of our system, was at first merely the dark centre of the great nebula, gradually becoming luminous, in one of its outer shells at least, and afterwards a solid or a liquid mass, surrounded by an atmosphere so dense that no ray could pass through it. But now on the fourth day its formation is completed, and it really appears as a luminary in the heavens; and therefore its formation is described as a part of that day's work, or, more correctly speaking perhaps, is described under the head of that day, just as we have already observed

[1] It is not meant to imply here that all the stars changed from nebulæ into liquid or solid spheres at the same time with our sun; nor does our record say so. Some would sooner attain to maturity, and some would require a longer time, while others may not have reached that stage even yet. As they are mentioned in the fourth day, however, that was probably the time at which most of them came to maturity.

that the creation of the vegetable world is described
on that day in which vegetable life was most fully
displayed, although there was a new creation of
plants on each of the three subsequent days; and,
as we shall afterwards have occasion to notice, just
as the creations of the different classes of animals
are described on those days in which they severally
appeared in the greatest numbers and in the highest
perfection. There was, in fact, no sun, properly so
called, until the fourth day, nor any light-giving
moon.[1]

Returning from the heavens to the earth: on the
commencement of the fourth day (co-extensive with
the period of the New Red Sandstone) great convulsions had arisen on its surface,[2] from what cause
we know not, breaking and disturbing its now com-

----

[1] In this, it will been seen, I differ essentially from previous defen-
ders and expounders of Moses' account, as they believe the sun to
have been created on the first day, but not to have shone upon the
earth till the fourth; whereas the doctrine here maintained is, that
there was no sun at all on the first and second days, and no finished
luminary even on the third or the beginning of the fourth.

[2] 'During the Devonian and the Carboniferous eras, volcanic eruptions were by no means so abundant as when the Lower Silurian rocks
were accumulated. . . . . The close, however, of that period was
specially marked by ruptures of the crust of the earth, which, from
the physical evidences placed before us, must have extended over very
distant regions. Whatever may have been the previous changes, it
was then that the coal strata and their antecedent formations were
very generally broken up by upheavals into separate troughs and
basins, distorted by numberless powerful dislocations. . . . . Yet,
notwithstanding these physical changes, the animals and plants of the

paratively thick crust to an extent never again to be
experienced,[1] and turning up the horizontal strata,
which seemed to be laid as immovably as the
'everlasting hills.' This disturbance immediately
preceded the deposition of the Permian strata,
which form the lower half of the New Red Sandstone system. These strata were deposited in the
bed of the sea, in the same manner as those of the
Old Red Sandstone, and with a similar appearance,
although with a great difference in their fossil remains. From the one to the other, certain species
of plants and of animals have been gradually disappearing, and others taking their place; but now,
in the Permian formation, we have, we are informed,
'a comparative paucity of vegetable and of animal
life.' 'The mass of the organic remains of the Permian group,' says Sir Roderick Murchison,[2] 'con-
stitute a remnant only of the earlier animals. They
exhibit the last of the successive changes which
these creatures underwent before their final disap-
pearance. The dwindling away and extinction of
many of the types which were produced and multi-

Permian era, though chiefly of new species, are generically connected
with those of the preceding or Carboniferous epoch, whilst they are
almost wholly dissimilar to those of the next succeeding period, the
Trias.'—*Siluria*, ch. xiii. p. 308.

[1] That is, of course, as far as the earth's history has advanced in
our own times. There is no intention here even to guess at the future.

[2] *Siluria*, ch. xiii. p. 344.

plied during the anterior epochs, already announce the end of the long Palæozoic period.   In ascending above the highest of the Permian deposits, the geologist takes indeed a sudden and final leave of nearly everything in nature to which the words *Primary, Primeval,* or *Palæozoic* have been applied.' Then what has now become of those grand forests and jungles which covered the earth in so rich profusion during the Carboniferous period?   They are almost entirely gone, and fields of coal have ceased to be deposited.   Geologists have failed to inform us what was the cause of so wonderful a change; but the remarkable passage of Scripture which is now under our consideration, along with the hypothesis on which we have hitherto built, may throw some light on the subject.

The surface of the earth, with its dense atmosphere now cleared, was rapidly cooling ; and to such an extent had this reached, that some of our latest geological observers have detected, on the boulders found imbedded among the Permian rocks, the first marks of glacial action recorded in the earth's history.[1]   There was no longer that great terrestrial heat and that dense warm atmosphere which made the plants rush up as if in a hothouse ; but the climate was assuming more and more of a

[1] For particulars regarding the grounds on which this statement is supported, see Note H.

wintery character.[1] Vegetation languished, and almost disappeared; the seas also cooled, and animal life was everywhere diminishing in number and in vigour. What was the key to all this? While the warmth supplied from the earth's interior was disappearing, although greater than it is now, there was as yet no sun to keep up the temperature of the surface. Animal and vegetable life would soon have wholly disappeared,[2] but for the next wonderful display of creative power,—that which we have already described. The remedy was provided ages before the need of it appeared, but is now fully ready. At the close of the Permian period the sun shone forth to restore perishing nature,—at first feebly, but, before the termination of the fourth day, in all its splendour.

If the sun shone upon earth for the first time, as Moses asserts that it did, on the fourth day, it ought to have left some record in nature sufficient to show to succeeding ages the all-important change which then took place. The plants and animals best adapted to flourish in a steaming atmosphere of an invariably high temperature would not be equally well adapted to the new state of things,—namely, a comparatively dry atmosphere, and great vicissitudes of temperature, in transitions from day to

[1] For further remarks on this, see Note K.
[2] As it would disappear now, if the solar heat were withdrawn.

night, and from summer to winter. The probability
is, that they could not survive the change. The
supporters of the theory of unlimited development
would say, that the old races of plants and of
animals would gradually accommodate themselves
to the altered state of circumstances, if such an
altered state there was, and would change with
them:

'Tempora mutantur et nos mutamur in illis.'

But they did no such thing. The rocks show us
no traces whatever of any such gradual transition at
that period. A totally new creation was required.
Accordingly we find that, in the transition from the
Permian to the Triassic system, which comes next
in order, although the change was attended by no
excessive volcanic activity, and by no unusual com-
motions, not even by any decided change in the
position or character of the strata, organic life
underwent a complete and a sudden renovation.
Previous to that transition there was little change
in either the animal or the vegetable world except
gradual decay; but immediately that we enter on
the Trias, the transition is already complete. 'The
fauna and flora of the Permian rocks,' says Murchison,[1] 'are essentially Palæozoic; for, whilst in a
great measure they are specifically distinct from
those of the Carboniferous system, the amount of

[1] *Siluria*, ch. xiii. p. 336.

agreement in the two groups is surprising, when we reflect upon the phenomena adverted to in the opening of this chapter, of great physical revolutions which pretty generally affected the known surface of the earth at or before the close of the preceding or Carboniferous era. These disruptions, therefore, however violent and extensive, were not universal, but were, we may suppose, so accompanied by new physical conditions[1] as to occasion the destruction of many plants and animals;' whereas the change from the Permian to the Triassic period was altogether different: for, as the same eminent author adds, in another part of his work,[2] 'At the close of the Permian or Supra-carboniferous era an infinitely greater change took place in organic life than that which marked the ascent from the Silurian system to the overlying Palæozoic groups. Nearly, if not quite, all the species of the earlier races then disappeared, and were replaced in the Trias by a new series, the types of which were continued through those long epochs which geologists term Secondary or Mesozoic.'[3]

No doubt the creations of animals to re-people the earth did not take place on a great scale till the

[1] The new physical condition, as we have already seen, appears to have been the advent of a period of great cold.

[2] *Siluria*, ch. xi. p. 481.

[3] Hugh Miller, speaking of the *Cycadaceæ*, an order of plants unknown in the coal-measures, says: 'One of the first known genera

fifth and sixth days; but the change was *begun* suddenly, in the middle of the fourth day, and by that time all, or almost all, the older species had disappeared.

In the next place, we know that, in our own times, vegetation is very different in the different zones of the earth. The trees and plants of the torrid zone are entirely different from those of the temperate zones, and these again from the few dwarfish specimens found in the Arctic regions. But in the Carboniferous period the most luxuriant vegetation flourished probably to the very poles,— and *that* consisting of the same kinds of plants and trees as those which are now found only in the warmest regions of the earth, while no marked difference has ever been observed in the character of the plants of which the coal strata have been formed in different latitudes. 'This earliest luxuriant tree vegetation,' says Murchison, 'the pabulum of our coal-fields, is also remarkable for its spread over many latitudes; and together with it occur the same common species of marine shells, all indicating a more or less equable climate from polar to inter-

of this curious order—the genus *Pterophyllum*—appears in the Trias. It distinctively marks the commencement of the Secondary flora, and intimates that the once great Palæozoic flora, after gradually waning throughout the Permian ages, and becoming extinct at their close, had been succeeded by a vegetation altogether new.'—*Testimony of the Rocks*, Lecture Twelfth, p. 475.

tropical regions,—a phenomenon wholly at variance with the present distribution of animal and vegetable life over the surface of the planet.'[1] Coals are as *abundant* in the coldest regions of the earth as in the hottest.

Since we know, then, that the unequal incidence of the solar rays is the great cause of the extreme inequality which now exists in the temperatures of the different latitudes, and since we cannot even imagine any way in which the climates of the polar and equatorial regions could be brought into agreement unless by the entire exclusion of the sun's rays, it follows that the sun either did not exist, or did not shine on the earth, during the Carboniferous era. And if we can determine the time at which the inequality of climates first arose, we also determine the period of the sun's first appearance in the heavens ; and since we have no evidence whatever of the existence of an equable temperature after the Permian era—and we know that the close of that era was coincident with the great change which then arose in the animal and vegetable world—we may naturally infer that that was the very epoch of the sun's first appearance.

Then, again, since we know that if the sun were

[1] *Siluria*, ch. xx. p. 479. Sir Roderick repeats this statement in many places, applying it to all the Palæozoic ages. (See pp. 488, 501, 502, etc.) Sir Charles Lyell also coincides with the above ; but for his remarks, and some comments upon them, see Note L.

to disappear now, the cold would be so great that
everything that grows or lives would perish, there
must have been some other source of the great
warmth which prevailed in the previous ages; and
we know of no other such source than the heat of
the ground. Even that would not have preserved
vegetation with a dry air and a clear sky. But
the humidity to which it would give rise, and to
which the peculiar vegetation of the coal period
testifies, would be the means of retaining that heat
in our atmosphere. But if the only source of
warmth was the ground, that, however dense the
atmosphere, must have been from age to age continually cooling; and if so, we have a strong
corroboration of the generally received theory of
the existence of a still higher terrestrial temperature in times still more remote.[1]

To sum up, then, in a few words, what I have
already said in regard to the remarkable epoch at
which we have arrived. At that epoch, without any
convulsions among the strata which might suggest a
terrestrial origin of the revolution which took place,
we find a sudden transition from one kind of plants
to another entirely different—so much so, that not a
single species remains the same; and we find also a
change from a tropical vegetation, extending from
pole to pole, to one diversified with plants suited to

[1] See Notes M and N.

every different latitude—some adapted to the excessive heat of the tropics, and capable of growing in that alone, others suited to the milder temperature of the middle latitudes, and to that alone ; and then, as we approach the poles, a vegetation becoming more and more scanty, till we arrive at nothing more than a few mosses and stunted willows, instead of the palms, araucarias, and tree-ferns which in the previous age grew luxuriantly, probably to the very highest latitudes. If this wonderful revolution is not to be explained by the introduction of solar heat and light, with the diversified climates which would be the necessary result, geologists, after much hard labour, have failed to assign any other adequate cause ; whereas, if the introduction of a solar orb into our firmament[1] was really the key to the solution of the mystery, here is certainly again a marvellous coincidence in our two records. Such coincidences could hardly be by chance, and still less can we fancy that they arose from Moses' geological knowledge, although he 'was learned in all the wisdom of the Egyptians.' We can hardly conceive how they could occur at all, unless from the fact that the true author of the first chapter of Genesis was also the creator of the rocks, and the

---

[1] It may be observed *en passant*, that we can hardly avoid the use of this word, even now that we have so copious a scientific language, although we have no belief in its *firmness*.

writer, on their own durable material, of their wonderful history.

Again it is said, 'God saw that it was good.' Who can doubt it? A glorious sun at last illuminates and cheers his fair creation, giving rise to all the pleasing vicissitudes of day and night, of summer and winter, of sunshine and shade, and also of calms and of storms; and itself the emblem of a greater sun, the 'Sun of Righteousness,' which was afterwards to shine still more gloriously in the spiritual firmament, rescuing the moral nature of man from a condition as hopeless as that from which the material sun now rescued the material creation. At the same time, an ever-changing moon for the first time throws its silvery rays over sea and land, over stream and lake, over mountain and valley, over pasture and forest.

'And the evening and the morning were the fourth day.'—GEN. I. 19.

The evening was gloomy indeed. The warmth of the earth, which had hitherto been the sole source of its teeming vegetation, was slowly but steadily disappearing. Winter came on colder and colder, and with no reviving spring. The snows, which at first had only whitened the tops of the highest mountains, steadily descended, driven back only in insulated spots by scattered volcanic fires. Glaciers fill the upland valleys, from the equator to the poles. The animal races are fast diminishing in numbers, many species going entirely out of existence, never to reappear; and the grand luxuriant forests, with their gorgeous flora, droop and die. Even the angels are all but dismayed, and exclaim, 'What next?' Some perhaps lose their faith for ever, and some look on in solemn awe, waiting to see by what unimaginable means our all-wise Creator can restore his now ruined world. But now comes the first dawn of morning. A red ball seems to move across the sky, but so faint in its light, and so hazy, that the eyes even of angels can hardly say whether it is a reality or an optical delusion. After doing so many thousands of times, it is clearly perceptible that it is an actual luminous orb. At last its rays perceptibly illuminate the mountain-tops, and finally dispel the mists, and throw a genial warmth on the plains below. The snow melts. The glaciers retire to the mountain-tops, and to the distant poles. Vegetation anew begins, but only begins, to gladden the valleys,[1] though with a foliage never seen before. A few large reptiles stalk along the shores, some unknown birds leave their footprints there also, and

[1] From whatever cause it may have arisen, there can be no doubt of the fact, that the Triassic flora is one extremely limited both in numerical amount and variety of species.—PAGE'S *Advanced Textbook of Geology,* art. 232.

a very few marsupial quadrupeds for the first time appear, and that only *at the close* of the fourth day.

But, altogether, the land animals (reptiles perhaps excepted) are almost as few as the trees and plants.[1] The seas, however, are more abundant in life; for while nearly all the bone-encased fishes have disappeared, and the heterocercal families have given place to the homocercal, and these in considerable variety, there are also shell-fishes in something like abundance, and a few crustaceans. But even in these there is an almost universal change.

In hasty review we have passed from darkness faintly broken by volcanic fires, from a cold and convulsed earth to the bright sunshine of a peaceful day, and from a cheerless, misty atmosphere, to a serene sky, with sun, moon, and stars. We have also passed figuratively from the gloom of a world in which life and vegetation were steadily dying out, to one in which there was a creation of new races to supply their place. For *the evening and the morning were the fourth day.*

---

[1] 'In the animal world, though the era (the Triassic) is marked by the introduction of new and higher forms, it by no means exhibits either extensive distribution, numerical amount, or variety of species. How and why this paucity of life, geology is yet unable to determine.' —*Ibid.* art. 231.

Perhaps the reader may think that the nebular hypothesis and its necessary consequences have now resolved the difficulty which hitherto has baffled geology.

It may be thought that less work has been done on earth on the fourth than on previous days; and the appearance is probably in accordance with the truth. But here again our records are harmonious. Geology speaks of *little*, and Moses has not thought it necessary even to take notice of *any*. His attention is altogether drawn away from it, to the wonderful metamorphosis going on in the heavens. The crust of the earth had become solidified; its roughnesses had been to a certain extent obliterated; never-melting ice for a while preserved the earth from any action but its own; the streams flowed perhaps less muddy than before, and the strata were more slowly accumulated. Still, in the Permian and Triassic formations together, a considerable thickness was added to the stratified crust of the earth.

CHAPTER V.

THE FIFTH DAY.

'And God said, Let the waters bring forth abundantly the moving creature that hath life, and fowl that may fly above the earth in the open firmament of heaven. And God created great whales, and every living creature that moveth, which the waters brought forth abundantly, after their kind, and every winged fowl after his kind : and God saw that it was good. And God blessed them, saying, Be fruitful, and multiply, and fill the waters in the seas, and let fowl multiply in the earth.'—GEN. 1. 20-22.

THE moving creature is translated, in the margin of the Bible, the creeping creature, which seems to be generally acknowledged to be the true rendering of the word, and is likely to be so, for the creation of quadrupeds is yet to come. This, then, as the rocks assuredly bear witness, was truly the age of creeping things ; for we are now come to the time of the Jurassic system, including the Oolitic and Liassic formations,—a system which, above all others, abounds in reptiles, and in these perhaps above all other living creatures,—so much so, that it has been named peculiarly *the age of reptiles.*

No doubt there were a few in previous systems; but as astronomers, when they want to determine the exact periodic time of a meteoric shower, do not take, as the period of its appearance, either the beginning of the shower or the end of it, but observe carefully the time of the greatest frequency of the meteors,—the hour in which the greatest number are seen,—the very same appears to be Moses' method in this and in other instances. He assigns to any class of creatures the day in which they appear in the greatest numbers and in the highest perfection. 'The oldest known reptiles,' Mr. Miller remarks,[1] 'appear just a little before the close of the Old Red Sandstone. . . . What seems to be the upper Old Red of our own country, has furnished the remains of a small reptile, equally akin to the lizards and the batrachians; and what seems to be the upper Old Red of the United States has exhibited the foot-tracks of a larger animal of the same class. . . . . In the coal-measures the reptiles hitherto found are all allied, though not without a cross of the higher crocodilian or lacertian nature, to the batrachian order,—that lowest order of the reptiles to which the frogs, newts, and salamanders belong. . . . . It was not, however, until the Permian and Triassic systems had come to a close, and even the earlier ages of the Oolitic system had passed away, that the class received its fullest development in creation. And certainly very wonderful was the development which it did then

[1] *The Testimony of the Rocks*, Lecture Second.

receive. Reptiles became everywhere the lords and
masters of this lower world. When any class of the
air-breathing vertebrates is very largely developed,
we find it taking possession of all the three old
terrestrial elements,—earth, air, and water. . . . .
Now, in the times of the Oolite, it was the reptilian
class that possessed itself of all the elements. Its
gigantic *enaliosaurs*, huge reptilian whales mounted
on paddles, were the tyrants of the ocean, and must
have reigned supreme over the already reduced
class of fishes ; its *pterodactyles*, dragons as strange
as were ever feigned by the romance of the middle
ages, and that, to the jaws and teeth of the crocodile, added the wings of a bat and the body and
tail of an ordinary mammal, had the " power of the
air," and pursuing the fleetest insects in their flight,
captured and bore them down ; its lakes and rivers
abounded in crocodiles and fresh-water tortoises of
ancient type and fashion ; and its woods and plains
were the haunts of a strange reptilian fauna of what
has been termed "fearfully great lizards,"—some of
which, such as the iguanodon, rivalled the largest
elephant in height, and greatly more than rivalled
him in length and bulk. Judging from what remains, it seems not impossible that the reptiles of
this Oolitic period were quite as numerous individu-
ally, and consisted of well-nigh as many genera and
species, as all the mammals of the present time. In

the cretaceous ages, this class, though still the dominant one, is visibly reduced in standing ; it had reached its culminating point in the Oolite, and then began to decline ; and with the first dawn of the Tertiary division, we find it occupying, as now, a very subordinate place in creation.'

It seems strange to every reader that the *waters* should bring forth *fowls ;* but it has been suggested of late years, that the word *fowls* in this verse should rather be translated *winged reptiles ;* and if so, the statement is quite in accordance, as we have just seen, with the evidence of geological records.[1]

For the statement that the *waters* produced reptiles of any kind, we can, of course, have no positive confirmation from Geology ; but from the facts that their skeletons are found in such numbers in strata deposited from water, and that some of them were provided with fins or paddles, we learn that their haunts were among the waters, or on the muddy shores, and probably also among the reedy swamps.

If, however, such was the true meaning of the word translated *fowl* in the twentieth verse, I have not heard it suggested that the word rendered *fowl* in the twenty-second verse should be similarly altered, and there is no reason from the context that

[1] I confess myself utterly ignorant of Hebrew, and I cannot now remember the authority for this suggested correction of our translation. But if it rests on no sufficient ground, the point is immaterial to the general scope of the argument.

G

it should be so.   In the latter verse fowls are mentioned in no connection with the sea, and we may
naturally understand that birds are meant.   We do
not, indeed, find many remains of birds in the strata
of this period ; but assuredly they are not found
at any earlier ; and I am not aware that they are
found more abundantly in the rock-formations of
any subsequent age, unless perhaps the Tertiary.
In fact, they appear, in general, to be very scarce.
Their thin and light bones would not sink in water,
if by any chance they fell into it, and could not
therefore be imbedded in the subjacent mud ; nor, if
thrown on a moist shore, would they be the kind of
bones most capable of preservation, while land-birds
would not even leave the impressions of their feet
on the shores.   The footprints of birds, however,
are found in strata not older than the upper Lias,
but only those of the *Grallæ*, or stilt order of birds ;
and their bones in the cretaceous system, which
also, according to our chronology, belongs to the
fifth day.

As to the *great whales* of the twenty-first verse,
we cannot depend upon the translation.   In fact, it
is not easy to understand why our translators so
rendered it, as the Hebrews could have no knowledge of the whale, and therefore no word for it.
In the margin it is *great sea-monsters ;* and these
assuredly there were in the Oolitic age, such as

those to which allusion has been made in our last quotation.

'And the evening and the morning were the fifth day.'—GEN. I. 23.

It will be understood, from what has been said above, that the fifth day, according to the views here set forth, comprehended the geological periods of the Oolitic and the Cretaceous systems. What the evening and the morning of this day were, does not clearly appear. It may be meant that, at its commencement, the solar atmosphere was but imperfectly cleared, and only a dim twilight fell upon the earth ; but at its close the sun shone out in all its brightness, and restored once more a high temperature to the earth,—not so high as it was in the Carboniferous and preceding ages, but still a tropical heat even in the middle latitudes.[1] Or it may signify that the earth, thinly clothed with vegetation, and peopled with few living creatures at the commencement of the day, as we know that it was at the close of the previous, presented, before the termination of this day, all the cheerfulness of revived vegetation and of active animal life : for the formation of coal-fields, interrupted on the previous day, is again renewed, and testifies to the revival of vegetation ; while the numerous remains of animals still preserved in the rocks of the period declare

[1] For the authorities on which this statement rests, see Note O.

that God's command in the twenty-second verse, 'Be fruitful and multiply,' was well obeyed.

If our readers are dissatisfied with both of these explanations of 'the evening and the morning of the fifth day,' I can only reply that there is much that is unknown to us yet. Geological research has not filled up all the details of the earth's history. We are not therefore called upon to explain every statement in the first chapter of Genesis. All that is demanded of us is to show that there is nothing in that chapter contradictory to the discoveries of science, but that all its announcements are in harmony with those discoveries *as far as they have as yet advanced.*

CHAPTER VI.

THE SIXTH DAY.

'And God said, Let the earth bring forth the living creature after his kind, cattle and creeping thing, and beast of the earth after his kind : and it was so. And God made the beast of the earth after his kind, and cattle after their kind, and every creeping thing that creepeth upon the earth after his kind : and God saw that it was good.'—GEN. L 24, 25.

THE fifth day seems to have ended at the close of the Cretaceous system, leaving the Tertiary period for the sixth day ; and accordingly Genesis and Geology both inform us that, at the commencement of that day, there was a new creation of animal life. 'Between the uppermost member of the Secondary series, and the oldest of the newer class of formations called Tertiary,' says Sir Charles Lyell, 'there is a remarkable discordance, as to species, of organic remains ; none having yet been found common to both.'[1]

---

[1] *Principles of Geology*, book i. ch. viii. After this statement, Sir Charles proceeds to describe the change of climate which has previously been spoken of, and then goes on to say, that 'alteration of climate must have been accompanied by geographical changes, the channels of seas being raised into tracts of dry land, and even high mountain chains, such as the Pyrenees, being thrown up, although

For this we may also take the evidence of the author we have so often quoted : [1]—'The curtain drops over this ancient flora of the Oolite in Scotland ; and when, long after, there is a corner of the thick enveloping screen withdrawn, and we catch a partial glimpse of one of the old Tertiary forests of our country, all is new. Trees of the high dicotyledonous class, allied to the plane and the buckthorn, prevail in the landscape, intermingled, however, with dingy, funereal yews ; and the ferns and equisetæ that rise in the darker openings of the wood approach to the existing type.'

Both Genesis and Geology also inform us that, during the sixth or Tertiary period, 'God made the beast of the earth after his kind, and cattle after their kind ;' for no rocks older than the Tertiary contain the remains of any mammalia except a few marsupials, which, as Mr. Miller shows,[2] are not

not to their entire present elevation.' Then, at p. 212 : 'The remarkable break above alluded to, between the most modern of the known Secondary rocks and the oldest Tertiary, may be in some measure apparent only, and ascribable to the deficiency of our information. . . . Nevertheless it is far from impossible that the interval between the Chalk and Tertiary formations constituted an era in the earth's history, when the transition from one class of organic beings to another was, comparatively speaking, rapid.' This is a wonderful admission from a geologist whose leading principle is the absence of catastrophes, and the continuance of events now as they have always been.

[1] Hugh Miller, *Testimony of the Rocks*, Lecture Twelfth.

[2] For his ingenious and original remarks on this point, see the *Testimony of the Rocks*, Lecture Second, p. 91.

true mammalia, but, as it were, an intermediate class between them and birds, and these so very insignificant in number, that, even regarding them as 'beasts of the earth,' it would have been utterly below the dignity of the Scripture narrative to describe them as characteristic of the day.[1] Geology assuredly bears witness that never before this period did the earth behold any of the carnivorous wild beasts which now roam through our forests, or of those herbivorous mammalia which feed wild upon the pastures of our grassy mountains and plains, such as deer, antelopes, buffaloes, hares, and rabbits, or of those domestic animals which are so familiar and so useful to us now. The cow which brings us milk, the sheep which gives us clothing, the horse which ploughs our fields and draws our carriages, the dog which watches our houses, keeps our sheep, and is our faithful attendant, and the cat, the playmate of our children, were unknown before this era. Such animals had no existence before the *sixth day*, says or implies our written record ; and such animals had no existence before the *Tertiary period*, the

[1] 'In the Stonesfield slate the remains of reptiles have been found associated with marine shells, and with them the jaws of at least two species of small mammiferous quadrupeds of a genus allied to the Didelphys or Opossum. It is very remarkable that these fossils afford the only exception yet known to the apparent absence of all terrestrial mammalia from the islands and continents which existed anteriorly to the Eocene period.'—*Principles of Geology*, book iv. ch. xxiii.

record of the rocks replies. Let any impartial
reader say if the coincidence is not again remarkable, or if it could be by chance.

As to the clause which follows, regarding 'everything that creepeth upon the earth,' we are not told
that such reptiles were now created for the first
time; for the twentieth verse informed us that
many of them appeared on the fifth day, and that
statement we found amply confirmed by Geology.
But now new kinds of reptiles come into existence.
The huge and monstrous species which seem to
have revelled on the earth on the fifth day, as its
principal occupants, have disappeared, and have
been succeeded by other races less formidable in
their aspect, and claiming only a share—in fact, now
only a subordinate share—with multitudes of other
animals, in the occupation of the soil. Now, also, they
are no longer 'free of the three elements,' as on the
previous day; for although some are amphibious as
far as regards land and water, yet no reptiles in our
time wing their way through our atmosphere, and I
believe none such are found in the Tertiary strata.[1]

' And God said, Let us make man in our own image, after our likeness; and let them have dominion over the fish of the sea, and over

[1] Herodotus, no doubt, asserts the existence of winged serpents in
ancient times, but he never saw them; and their skeletons, which he
describes as still visible in Ethiopia, may really have been fossil
specimens, if they existed at all.

the fowl of the air, and over the cattle, and over all the earth, and
over every creeping thing that creepeth upon the earth. So God
created man in his own image : in the image of God created he him ;
male and female created he them. And God blessed them : and God
said unto them, Be fruitful, and multiply, and replenish the earth,
and subdue it ; and have dominion over the fish of the sea, and over
the fowl of the air, and over every living thing that moveth upon the
earth.'—GEN. I. 26-28.

Here was, at last, the completion of God's great
work of creation, the hewing out and the placing of
the keystone of the arch. Here was now the reward
given to the angels who had looked on in patience,
and for so many millions of years waited with sted-
fast faith for the final development of the grand
scheme. Now 'the morning stars sang together, and
the sons of God shouted for joy.' Now, it may be,
those whose faith had failed were deeply mortified,
and conspired to destroy God's glorious work. Now
had appeared on earth a creature—not with his eyes
turned earthward, but with his visage erect,—not
with instincts limited to the supply of daily food and
shelter, but with an understanding capable of search-
ing into all science, and recording all history, investi-
gating all the wonders of the sublunary creation, in
its mineral, its vegetable, and its animal kingdoms,
and in its aërial heights and its oceanic depths,
leaving no dark corner unexplored,—not satisfied
with the things of earth, but aspiring to a knowledge
of the heavens above, fathoming their depths, mea-
suring and weighing their great orbs, tracing their

complicated movements, and not limited to the observation of facts, but attempting to reach their
causes. Here was formed at last the only one of
the earth's inhabitants conscious of the existence of
a Creator, and capable of adoring and serving him.
Now was attained the perfection of that pattern
which the great Creator of all things seems to have
had in view from the first formation of living things,
and to which he more and more nearly approached
as creation advanced.[1]

If the words, ' Let us make man in our own image,
after our own likeness,' are correctly rendered, then,
in as far as finity could resemble infinity, in as far
as the fallible could be an image of the infallible,
here was man, in all his intellectual powers and in
all his moral sentiments resembling his Creator,
following his modes of reasoning, imitating him,
though unintentionally, in the application of his own
laws,[2] and conforming to his moral restraints. But
this is probably not all that is meant by the expression 'in our image.' It has been said that the more
correct translation would be '*for* our image,' meaning,
for a model of the form in which the Son of God
was afterwards to appear on earth. But whether

---

[1] For this idea I am again indebted to Mr. Miller ; but the passage
I cannot bring to my recollection, nor even the volume in which it
appears.

[2] For some beautiful illustrations of this, see the *Testimony of the
Rocks*, Lecture Sixth.

this be a more correct interpretation or not, it seems clear that man was formed in the likeness, not of God the Father, but of God the Son—in that form which he was at a later period to assume visibly to men. Then the likeness was completed not in intellect and moral sentiments merely, but even in corporeal frame.

• It was, not improbably, in the assumption of the intellectual form of the man who was to be, that the Deity carried on the whole work of creation,[1] and thereby it appeared so much like the work of a human architect, only of infinitely higher wisdom and power, that the contrivances of creation, if they may be so called, resembled the contrivances of man, and that the whole scheme of science is so arranged as to be adapted in every respect to the peculiar faculties of man and to his modes of investigation, as if courting, assisting, and sanctioning his inquiry. If such a view is correct, it amounts to this: that God created the universe with the intellect of a man, and therefore his work is intelligible to man.

In the expression, 'male and female created he them,' some critics have professed to find a contra-diction of the subsequent account of the creation of woman in the second chapter. Even if, however, her separate formation was not completed till after the sixth day, yet the germ of her form, and even of

[1] See John i. 3, 4.

her life, might have been latent in the side of Adam. But if any think this incredible, they are at liberty to do so, for I rest nothing upon it except as a mere suggestion of a possibility. A more probable explanation is this,—that, although the particulars of Eve's formation are not given till after the account of the seventh day, it does not follow that it did not take place before that day; for all that follows the third verse in the second chapter has every appearance of being a *resumé* of the narrative of the first chapter, which was cut short in order to introduce the notice of the seventh day's rest. Otherwise we should have a second creation of the beasts of the earth and of the fowls of the air, as mentioned in the nineteenth verse of the second chapter, and that in the very midst of the account of the origin of Eve.

The Bible narrative is here again wonderfully supported by geological records; for we have no fossil relics of man found in any even of the Tertiary strata,[1] which contain numerous specimens of the somewhat older mammalia, much less in any of the previous formations. The only fossil remains of the human species that have been found, were in recent travertine, in gravel of a late date, in caves of an

---

[1] The exact time of man's appearance on earth, in geological history, is now generally admitted to have been at the close of the glacial period.

equally modern origin, or in still more recent peat mosses.[1]

'And God said, Behold, I have given you every herb bearing seed, which is upon the face of all the earth, and every tree, in the which is the fruit of a tree yielding seed ; to you it shall be for meat. And to every beast of the earth, and to every fowl of the air, and to every thing that creepeth upon the earth, wherein there is life, I have given every green herb for meat : and it was so.'—GEN. I. 29, 30.

Now, when Genesis and Geology no longer concur in testifying to the same fact, they do that which is equivalent : they bear witness to the different parts of the same fact, their respective testimonies dovetailing into each other. Genesis says that now God gave to man, for food, every tree in which is the fruit of a tree yielding seed. Now, what are the fruits which man finds good for food, and in which he peculiarly delights? Without going beyond the bounds of our own island, we know that they are apples, pears, plums, cherries, berries, and nuts of various kinds, peaches, apricots, and grapes. Then, turning to ask what Geology says, we read

'I need not dwell,' says Sir Charles Lyell, 'on the proofs of the low antiquity of our species, for it is not controverted by any experienced geologist ; indeed, the great difficulty consists in tracing back the signs of man's existence on the earth to that comparatively modern period when species now his contemporaries began to predominate. If there be a difference of opinion respecting the occurrence in certain deposits of the remains of man and his works, it is always in reference to strata confessedly of the most modern order ; and it is never pretended that our race co-existed with assemblages of animals and plants of which all, or even a great part, of the species are extinct.'—*Principia of Geology*, book I. ch. ix.

these words, or intimations to the same effect:
'These fruits may be given to man *now*, for the
earth produces them all abundantly; but before the
Tertiary period, that is, the sixth day, they could
not even have been offered to man: for, as far as
the evidence of the rocks goes, they had before that
day no existence, nor do they appear to have come
into existence till about the close of that day, just
before man himself was made to cultivate and to
enjoy them.' The garden which Adam was to
'dress and to keep' appears, from both records
alike, to have been planted almost contemporaneously with Adam's own appearance on the stage.
The same thing may be said of the different kinds
of grain, if they are included under the general
terms of the twenty-sixth verse, and also, I believe,
of all our garden vegetables. Immediately after
the residence was well stored with all kinds of food
for sustenance and enjoyment, the arrival of its
occupant was announced. Then, as to the lower
animals, they also now have nutriment on which
they can live and thrive, while that was probably
not the case until the last day of creation. There is
no probability, for instance, that our mammalia
could have lived on the vegetation of the Carboniferous era, luxuriant though it was. 'We know
generally,' says the author on whose statements
and opinions we have so often rested with satis-

faction,[1] 'that with each successive period there appeared a more extensively useful and various vegetation than that which had gone before. I have already referred to the sombre and unproductive character of the earliest terrestrial flora with which we are acquainted. It was a flora unfitted, apparently, for the support of either graminivorous bird or herbivorous quadruped. The singularly profuse vegetation of the coal-measures was, with all its wild luxuriance, of a resembling cast. So far as appears, neither flock nor herd could have lived on its greenest and richest plains. Nor does even the flora of the Oolite seem to have been in the least suited for the purposes of the shepherd or herdsman. Not until we enter on the Tertiary periods do we find floras amid which man might have profitably laboured as a dresser of gardens, a tiller of the fields, or a keeper of flocks and herds. Nay, there are whole orders and families of plants, of the very first importance to man, which do not appear till late in even the Tertiary ages. Some degree of doubt must always attach to merely negative evidence; but Agassiz, a geologist whose opinions must be received with respect by every student of the science, finds reason to conclude that the order of the Rosaceæ—an order more important to the gardener than almost any other, and to

[1] Mr. Miller, in *The Testimony of the Rocks*, Lecture First, p. 44.

which the apple, the pear, the quince, the cherry,
the plum, the peach, the apricot, the victorine, the
almond, the raspberry, the strawberry, and the
various brambleberries belong, together with all the
roses and the potentillas—was introduced only a
short time previous to the appearance of man. And
the true grasses—a still more important order,
which, as the corn-bearing plants of the agricul-
turist, feed at the present time at least two-thirds of
the human species, and in their humbler varieties
form the staple food of the grazing animals—scarce
appear in the fossil state at all. They are peculiarly
plants of the human period.'

Mr. Miller then speaks of another family, the
Labiate, of which no trace has been found even in
the Tertiary deposits,—a family producing neither.
luscious fruit nor very beautiful flowers, but yielding rich perfumes. It must have been introduced
at the close of the Tertiary period, immediately
before man's appearance. No wonder, then, all
things considered, that the verse which follows in
our written record commences as it does.

'And God saw everything that he had made, and, behold, it was
very good. And the evening and the morning were the sixth day.'—
GEN. I. 31.

Previously to this, it was said of each successive
stage in creation, merely that it was *good;* but
now it is pronounced more emphatically, when God

saw everything that he had made, that it was *very good.*

When the earth was fully prepared,—when the chaotic nebulæ had become solid globes,—when land and ocean had been assigned their separate localities, and thus become residences appropriate to their respective inhabitants, — when an atmosphere, with its ingredients mixed in due proportion for the sustenance of vegetable and of animal life, breathed refreshing breezes over both, and floated upon it fleecy clouds dropping genial showers,— when the intense heat of the earth had been cooled down till it became a rich nursery for a rank vegetation for future use,—when that heat had further subsided, and left the earth dependent for its main source of warmth on the great central orb,—when sun and moon brought round yearly, monthly, and daily, the interesting vicissitudes of summer and winter, of spring and autumn, and of days and nights, the latter alternating between darkness and moonshine,—when the strata which form the earth's crust were all built up, teeming with abundant stores as yet unexplored and unappropriated,— when the seas were peopled with fishes of genera and species more numerous and more varied than they had ever been before,—when the hills were covered with grass, pastured by flocks and herds, —when the vernal meadows were gay and fragrant

with flowers,—when the plains waved with the
yellow corn of summer, and the luscious fruits of
autumn were dropping from the trees in wasteful
profusion,—then at last appeared the head of God's
sublunary creation—he whom the Creator had ap-
pointed from the first to govern the earth and to
preside over all its inhabitants, not in the debase-
ment of savage life to which he was afterwards to
sink, not in the refined covetousness and duplicity
of a more civilised stage, not with the horrible
aspect of the warrior slaughtering the myriads of
his fellow-men in pursuit of that which Satan told
him was glory, but in his original innocence, and
with all his bodily powers and all his mental
faculties in full perfection,—those powers and
faculties with which he was ultimately to subdue
all nature, and to mould it in a great measure to his
will. No wonder that the Almighty Creator now,
when he saw everything that he had made, pronounced it VERY GOOD.

Rationalists tell us, according to the measure of
their wisdom, that prophecy and miracles were
alike impossible. Creation, however, was not only
a stupendous miracle, but, in all except the final
stage (if we even except that), it was a grand prophecy. I have previously spoken of the very coal-
fields being prophetic ; but so also in one sense was
all creation. For ages it wanted a head, and yet

without that head it was evidently incomplete. There were stores of all kinds laid up for some intellectual creature who did not as yet exist. Here were all the materials for his lodging, his clothing, his food, his enjoyment. Here was granite for his docks and bridges, sandstone for the walls of his houses, and marble for their inner adornments. Here was earth that could be made into bricks for his humbler abodes, timber for his ships and for his buildings, and lime for cement scattered everywhere. Even salt to give relish to his victuals was not forgotten, but deposited in basins here and there among the Triassic strata. In the crevices of the rocks were laid up gold, silver, copper, lead, tin, and other metals ; and not confined to crevices, but in profuse abundance in certain kinds of rock, was iron, because it would be required for the use of man more than any other metal. It was not by chance that sand lay scattered upon the shores, capable of easy conversion into transparent glass, —capable of being melted, blown, drawn out, moulded, cut, and adapted to such a variety of useful and refined purposes. Not only were carboniferous stores dormant in the bowels of the earth, which were after the lapse of ages to provide for him light, warmth, and motive power ; but magnetism lay dormant, which was to guide his ships,—galvanic electricity lay dormant, which was in the latter days to carry his messages with lightning speed. Science itself lay dormant, with boundless fields for its display, and inexhaustible stores for its use. It lay dormant because there was not yet an intellectual being to arouse it, with his magic wand, from its long sleep. Its stores of treasures were all accumulated, but no creature had as yet a key which could unlock the store-rooms. The very existence, however, of these stores was prophetic of one to whom that key was afterwards to be committed; and if we are to apply to this Jeremiah's test of true prophecy,[1] it well stands the test; for its fulfilment is now proclaimed by the theoretical investigations and the experimental researches of our men of science, by the variety and grandeur of their discoveries, and by the vast utility of the practical results of these. The transactions of our Philosophical Societies convey their united contributions towards the attestation of that fulfilment.

As the earth, the abode of man, has the best position among the planets for obtaining a view of all the members of the solar system, so in regard to time, the close of the sixth day of God's creation, the period which follows the laying down of the last

---

[1] 'When the word of the prophet shall come to pass, then shall the prophet be known, (that the Lord hath truly sent him.'—Jer. xxviii. 9.

of the Post-tertiary deposits is the commencement of the best age in which man could have been placed on his earthly abode, to obtain a view of God's entire plan in the structure of the earth,—the only age in which man could have studied the whole science of astronomy and of geology.

There is another matter, not yet noticed, in which the Book and the Rocks are in perfect harmony. The theory of *development* is not in itself absurd. On the contrary, it wears an outward aspect of nature and of truth. It is sufficiently plausible, and, if tried by our reasoning faculties alone, they could not have condemned it. But, in the first place, it labours under the unhappy disadvantage of being opposed to fact; for, as Mr. Miller has so clearly demonstrated in the *Footprints of the Creator*, every order of plants and of animals, as their petrified remains attest, appeared, in its first entrance on the world's stage, as perfect in its formation as any of the subsequent species of the same order; and no species underwent any material change during the whole time of its existence, but left the world as it entered into it. And again, in the rocky strata we nowhere find any plants or animals in a state of transition from one genus or from one species to another. Then it also labours under the additional disadvantage of being entirely opposed to the account which God himself has given us of his own work. In denying the development theory, the record written on the parchment of the Bible is in perfect harmony with the record written on the geologist's tables of stone.

'The evening and the morning were the sixth day.' We are not able to say very precisely in what form the evening and the morning of this day showed themselves; but we are informed by geologists that the period *had* an evening in which some unaccountable revolution again took place, all the previously existing species of animals and of plants dying away, and a morning in which a new race succeeded them. This change may have been accompanied by a transition from actual darkness to visible light unknown to us, for darkness can leave no impression on the rocks; but it is not necessary to the interpretation of the passage that it should have been so. As we render *a day* by a long period, just as freely may we understand a transition from evening to morning to signify one from commotion to tranquillity, — from destruction to construction, — from death to life.[1] 'In reviewing the facts above enumerated,' says Sir Charles

[1] In prophetic language, trouble is often represented by *darkness*, and tranquillity by *light*. Thus in Joel ii. 1, 2 : 'For the day of the Lord cometh, a day of clouds and of thick darkness.' In Isa. viii. 22 : 'And they shall look upon the earth, and behold trouble and darkness, dimness of anguish.' In Isa. xxx. 26 : 'The light of the moon shall be as the light of the sun, and the light of the sun shall be seven-

Lyell,[1] 'I may call attention to the important circumstance, that no species of fossil shell has yet been found common to the Secondary and Tertiary formations.' And 'this marked discordance in the organic remains of the two series is not confined to the testacea, but extends, so far as a careful comparison has yet been instituted, to all the other departments of the animal kingdom, and to the fossil plants.' The mere change from a world occupied by nothing higher than 'the brutes that perish,' to one inhabited by human beings with high mental faculties and immortal souls, might alone be called a transition from evening to morning.

I cannot conclude without asking the reader to take notice of an objection to the Bible narrative, made by no less acute a writer than Bishop Colenso, and to observe how ridiculous it appears when read in the light which I have, I trust successfully, attempted to throw upon that narrative. He wishes to show that the first and second chapters of Genesis are not harmonious, and, as the first instance of their disagreement, takes the following :[2] 'In the first, the earth emerges from the waters, and is therefore saturated with moisture, ch. i. 9,

fold, in the day that the Lord bindeth up the breach of his people.' And again, in Isa. lviii. 10 : 'Then shall thy light rise in obscurity, and thy darkness be as the noonday.'

[1] *Principles of Geology*, book iv. ch. xxiii.
[2] *The Pentateuch, &c., critically examined*, Part ii. p. 171.

10. In the second, the whole face of the ground requires to be moistened, ch. ii. 6.' According to the view I have taken, many millions of years intervened between the two events.

It is also objected that, since the seventh day could not have been a long period of time, but must have been a day of twenty-four hours, it would be an awkward mode of expression, altogether beneath the dignity of inspired language, to take six of the seven days as ages of immensely long duration, and the seventh as only a common day. Whatever the term *day* may stand for in the one case, it must evidently have its counterpart in the other. This is admitted; and our reply is, that the seventh day itself, as mentioned in the second chapter, is not a day of twenty-four hours, but is also a long period of time. Some light seems to be thrown upon this by our Saviour's expression, 'My Father worketh hitherto, and I work,'[1] implying that God's day of rest was beginning when the Christian dispensation commenced. This idea seems to be further illustrated in the Epistle to the Hebrews,[2] in which it is said: 'There remaineth, therefore, a rest to the people of God.' That day was probably begun when our Saviour's work of redemption began,[3]

[1] John v. 17.   [2] Heb. iv. 9.
[3] 'God's Sabbath of rest,' says Hugh Miller, 'may still exist; the work of Redemption may be the work of his Sabbath-day.'—*Footprints of the Creator*, Twelfth edition, p. 295.

that is, immediately after the creation of man,—its
evening extending over the antediluvian ages, the
patriarchal times, and the period of the Jewish dispensation ; its morning dawning at our Saviour's
resurrection ; and its fuller light being destined to
blaze forth in noonday splendour, when 'the kingdoms of the world are become the kingdoms of our
Lord and of his Christ,'[1]—when 'they shall not
hurt or destroy in all God's holy mountain,'[2]—when
'the earth shall be full of the knowledge of the
Lord, as the waters cover the sea,'[3]—when Satan,
bound and imprisoned for a thousand years, shall
'deceive the nations no more till the thousand years
shall be fulfilled.'[4]

[1] Rev. xi. 15.   [2] Isa. xi. 9.   [3] *Ibid.*
[4] Rev. xx. 2, 3. For further remarks on the subject, see Note P.

NOTES.

NOTE A, Page 38.

THERE are some questions to be answered, and some difficulties to be surmounted, before we can remove every objection to the Nebular Hypothesis, or fairly appreciate its
consequences.

A question which meets us at the outset is this: What was
the original constitution of the nebula in regard to the relative density of its different regions? Was it nearly alike, in
that respect, from centre to circumference, or was it more
dense towards the centre, and gradually shaded off towards
the exterior?

Before we can answer this question, we must have replies
to *two* others.

First.—*Supposing a spherical nebula to exist, of uniform
density, what would be the law of attraction of its component
molecules towards the common centre of gravity?*

Any molecule placed at the exterior would be attracted by
the entire mass of the nebula, as if the whole were accumulated
in the centre of gravity; but any molecule nearer the centre
would be attracted only by the spherical mass within the
range of its distance from the centre, the exterior shell having
no influence whatever upon it.

Every molecule would therefore be attracted towards the
centre with a force directly as the mass of the sphere within
its own distance from the centre, or directly as the cube of
that distance (since the density is uniform), and (in conse-

quence [1] of the usual law of gravity) inversely as the square of the same distance,—that is, taking the two ratios together, directly as the first power of its distance from the centre.

Second.—Supposing a spherical nebula [2] to exist, of uniform density, would it remain of uniform density, or would it become more dense in its interior than in its exterior regions?

To answer this,—let R and r represent the radii of two concentric spheres of the supposed nebula, and consequently $R^3 \times \frac{4}{3}\pi$ and $r^3 \times \frac{4}{3}\pi$ their contents. Then, since the attractive forces acting upon any two molecules at different distances from the centre would, as just proved, be directly as their distances from the centre, the spaces through which they moved under the influences of those forces in a given time, would also be directly as the same distances; and, in the same time in which all the molecules at the distance R were drawn nearer the centre by $\frac{1}{n}R$ (n being any number whatever), all those at the distance r would be drawn nearer by $\frac{1}{n}r$. In that time the radii of the two supposed spheres would be contracted by these proportionate parts of their lengths, and would become respectively $R \times \frac{n-1}{n}$ and $r \times \frac{n-1}{n}$, while their contents would be reduced to $R^3 \times \left(\frac{n-1}{n}\right)^3 \times \frac{4}{3}\pi$ and $r^3 \times \left(\frac{n-1}{n}\right)^3 \times \frac{4}{3}\pi$. The contents of the two spherical shells by which the two spheres were reduced, would be $R^3 \times \left\{1-\left(\frac{n-1}{n}\right)^3\right\} \times \frac{4}{3}\pi$ and $r^3 \times \left\{1-\left(\frac{n-1}{n}\right)^3\right\} \times \frac{4}{3}\pi$, two quantities which are to each other as the cubes of the radii.

Next,—to estimate the relative magnitudes of the two spaces

[1] This, with all that precedes it, is proved in the *Principia*, and is familiar to mathematicians.

[2] If irregular in form, the first change it would undergo would be to become spherical, unless in so far as its rotation might give it more or less of the spheroidal form.

into which the contents of these two shells have been compressed. By the time the *outermost* molecules of the outer shell have fallen in from the distance R to $R \times \frac{n-1}{n}$,—that is, by one *n*th part of the whole radius,—the *innermost* molecules of the same shell have also, as proved before, fallen through a space equal to one *n*th of their distance from the centre, or $\frac{1}{n}$ of $R \times \frac{n-1}{n}$. In like manner, the innermost molecules of the inner shell have approached the centre by the distance $\frac{1}{n}$ of $r \times \frac{n-1}{n}$. The thicknesses of the two shells, into which the materials of the two original shells have been compressed, are therefore to each other as R to r, and consequently have their contents in the ratio to each other of R^3 to r^3, since they are similar solids. But the contents of the two original shells, it has been shown, are to each other in the same ratio. Therefore the contents of the two original shells are compressed in the same proportion.

It follows from this, that if the supposed sphere was homogeneous in density at first, it would always continue to be so. But if the material of our planets were now distributed over the adjacent spherical (or spheroidal) shells next without them,[1] or over spherical (or spheroidal) shells of any extent, with widths proportional to the respective distances of the planets from the sun, the density of the nebula so made up would have no approximation to uniformity. The great nebula, therefore, could not at any time have been uniform in its density, and, *à fortiori*, it could not have been more dense in its exterior than in its interior regions, since it is now less so.

We may also perhaps be permitted to regard it as a corol-

[1] That is, supposing the material of each planet to have been collected from the shell between its own orbit and that of the next without it.

lary to the preceding demonstration, that if the matter of the nebula were originally greater in density towards the centre than in its exterior regions, as it must have been, the inequality would continually increase, until the materials of the different planets became separated.

But the proposition itself, and consequently any inference drawn from it, is demonstrated only in the case of a spherical nebula, while that we have seen would become more and more spheroidal, finally changing into separate rings. Our conclusions, however, will hold good for its earlier stage at all events; and it is only at that stage that we shall have occasion to apply them as far as regards light, while as far as regards heat it matters little whether they are true or not.

We may pause a moment here to point out that, on examining the results of the supposed distribution of the material of our present planets, there appear to have been originally *two great rings* in incipient formation, or formed, round the central nebulous mass, to be afterwards subdivided,—one of these containing the substance of the planets Mercury, Venus, the Earth, and Mars, and the other Jupiter, Saturn, Uranus, and Neptune; Venus, or rather its material, being in the densest part of the former, and Jupiter in that of the latter,—the material of the Asteroids occupying the intermediate space in a state of extreme rarity, even comparatively with the rest of the nebula.

The next point which claims our attention is this: The condensation of a gaseous medium would, of course, at once excite sensible heat; but as we have excluded such a medium from our hypothesis, a little difficulty arises: for, since we commence with a temperature of absolute zero, how are we to get our first dawn of heat, and the consequent production of a resisting medium? For it is conceded that heat could not arise from the mere descent of solid molecules, until their fall came to be impeded by some means.

Now the first change which would arise in the nebula as a whole, would be that of condensation, the molecules all approaching the centre, and drawing closer together; and unless we could suppose them to revolve in complete orbits round their common centre of gravity, returning to the same elevation from which they had fallen, the process of condensation would continue until collisions among them ensued. But all the conditions are wanting which in the solar system ensure the indefinite continuance of the movements without permanent disturbance, except revolution of all in one direction,— a condition which also, under the mutual perturbations of the molecules, would soon cease. Their orbits would not be circles, or make any approach to them : they would be in different planes, and there would be no grand controlling mass in the centre. The result would probably be a perfect dance in mazy orbits, and innumerable collisions. Collisions would excite heat, and heat would convert a portion of the molecules from a solid to a gaseous condition.

Let us hear the judgment of one of our highest authorities in astronomy on this subject. 'Among a crowd of solid bodies, of whatever size,' says Sir John Herschel, 'animated by independent and partially opposing impulses, motions opposite to each other must produce collision, destruction of velocity, and subsidence, or nearer approach towards the centre of preponderant attraction ; while those which conspire or remain outstanding after such conflicts, must ultimately give rise to circulation of a permanent character.' That is, of course, if there was a preponderance of rotatory motion in one direction at the outset. 'Whatever we may think of such collisions as events, there is nothing in their conception contrary to sound mathematical principles.'—*Outlines of Astronomy*, third edition, art. 872.

But if any one should still object that Sir John, notwithstanding his own words 'of whatever size,' has here in view bodies of some considerable bulk as the constituents of the supposed nebula, and that collisions among those that had no size greater than that of the ultimate atoms of matter would be all but impossible, I am not disposed to dispute the point ; for if there were not collisions, there would at least be approaches to within indefinitely small distances, accompanied by mutual revolutions of extreme rapidity ; and in the present state of our knowledge, who will say that such a condition of motion among the molecules is not itself the very essence of heat ? It has at least been maintained to be so by one school of philosophy. But whether or not, the atoms, approaching to so close a contiguity, will stop, or to a certain extent retard, each other's motions, and so produce heat.

However the difficulty may be resolved, its existence does not arise from any opposition that the present state of our knowledge presents to the hypothesis, but from the limited extent of that knowledge. It is not necessary that we should be able to clear away every difficulty, provided that we show that such difficulties do not militate directly or decidedly against our theory.

Assuming, then, that heat might originate from the condensa-tion of a nebula of solid atoms of matter, would that heat be great ? Would it be sufficient to bring the whole nebula from a temperature of absolute zero into a gaseous or even a liquid condition ? This, happily, is not a matter for conjecture, but, on certain conditions, for calculation.

From Mr. Joule's well-known experiments on heat, it appears that the number of foot-pounds of mechanical work which must be expended in order to raise the temperature of one pound of water one degree of Fahrenheit, is 772. If a quantity of water fell from a height of 772 feet, and then were stopped, it would excite as much heat as would be sufficient to raise its own temperature one degree, and the same for every 772 feet that it fell ; so that, in falling a mile, it would acquire a heating-power of about seven degrees. It matters not what may be the quantity of water that falls, as the result will be the same with an atom, a drop, or an ocean. But for any other substance than water, we must multiply the number of degrees by the number of times that the specific heat of that substance is contained in the specific heat of water.

All this, however, is applicable only to the case of bodies falling near the earth's surface, or under an attractive force equal to that which acts there. For any other force, the heat excited, or excitable, will be directly proportional to that force for the same distance fallen. Or, if we choose, we may estimate by velocity; the heat being always the same for the same velocity, whatever may be the accelerating force, but varying directly as the square of the velocity, where that varies. Our unit of velocity is found from the usual formula, $v^2 = 2fs$, to be 223 feet per second.

A fall of any extent, or any velocity attained, does not itself excite heat, but it gives the power of exciting the heat when the fall, or the velocity, is stopped by any mechanical means.

If we put F to represent the accelerating force of the attraction towards the centre of the nebula at the earth's present distance from it—say 92 millions of miles—and take the earth's diameter, in round numbers, as 8000 miles, and the mass of the nebula within the earth's distance as 400,000 times the mass of the earth itself, since it would be almost identical with the mass of the sun, we have $F = 32.2 \times 400,000 \times$

$$\left(\frac{4,000}{92,000,000}\right)^2 = .02435.$$

Next putting f to represent the accelerating force of the same attraction at any other point within the nebular shell, of whose materials the earth is to be formed, at the distance d from the centre, and disregarding any trifling difference which might be made by the attraction of the thin nebulous matter of that shell, we may take the force of gravitation as inversely proportional to the distance from the centre of the nebula, and consequently $f = \left(\frac{92,000,000}{d}\right)^2 \times F.$

Allowing H to denote the heating power in degrees, s the distance fallen in feet, and S the same in miles, v the velocity attained in feet per second, and V the same in miles per hour $\left(v \text{ being} = V \times \frac{44}{30}\right)$, then, from what was said before,

$$H = \left(\frac{v}{223}\right)^2 = \left(\frac{V}{223} \times \frac{44}{30}\right)^2, \text{ or } H = \frac{s}{772} \times \frac{f}{32.2} = \frac{S \times 5280}{772}$$
$$\times \frac{f}{32.2} = S \times .212f.$$

I

To ascertain, then, the heating power acquired by any molecule, or aggregation of molecules, in falling through a great distance, we may divide the distance into a number of equal parts,
severally so small that the accelerating force may be taken as
constant over any one part, and find, by the formula for f, the
accelerating forces due to the several distances. Then, by the
last formula for H, we may compute the heating power acquired
in falling through the respective distances. Finally, we may
take the sum of these, and divide it by the specific heat of the
substance, that of water being expressed as unity.

Supposing, then, the earth to have been collected from the
material of a nebulous shell, the innermost surface of which
was at double the distance which the earth is at present from
the centre, and the outermost at three times the same distance,
so that, in falling in to the present distance of the earth, the
nearest part would descend 92 millions of miles, and the
farthest part twice as far, or 184 millions,[1] and dividing the
latter distance into 46 equal stages, of 4 millions each, and the
nebula itself into 23 shells of equal thickness, we then compute
the heating power acquired by the material of each of these
shells in falling through its own number of stages to the earth's
present position, and that on the hypothesis that the several
shells would contain equal quantities of matter, the greater
bulk of the more distant compensating for their greater rarity.
For the accelerating force acting upon the falling material
during its passage through each of these shells, we may take,
as near enough for our purpose, the average between the forces
acting upon its inner and upon its outer surface.

By this mode of calculation, and on the various suppositions
laid down, we find that the average gain of heat-producing
power by the whole nebula, in consequence of its descent, is
281,690 degrees. But from this we have to deduct the heat-

---

[1] Of course these dimensions are merely hypothetical, but they are
by no means improbable if the nebular hypothesis has any sound
foundation ; and my object is to show that, sufficient dimensions being
allowed to the nebula, we obtain a heating power as great as can be
desired.

producing power still retained by the earth, in the form of velocity in its revolution round the sun. Now, without deducting anything from its present velocity to allow for its original velocity in rotation as a part of the nebula, since that velocity must have been very small,[1] we may take it, in round numbers, at 1100 miles per minute, or 66,000 miles per hour, or 96,800 feet per second; and that, from the formula $H = \left(\frac{v}{223}\right)^2$, gives $H = \left(\frac{96,800}{223}\right)^2 = 188,426$ degrees. Subtracting this from 281,690, we have 93,264 degrees for the heat which must actually have been acquired by the nebula, on the supposition that it consisted of water alone. But I think we shall be clear of every appearance of an over-estimate if we take the specific heat of the earth's actual material as only one-half that of water, and that will raise our actual temperature to 186,528 degrees of Fahrenheit, counted from zero absolute.

A still further increase would take place when the nebulous ring itself was broken and drawn together into a globular form. It may therefore safely be maintained that there is room enough, under our hypothesis, for as high a temperature as either astronomer or geologist can demand.

Note B, Page 41.

I have said, on page 41, that theoretical considerations show that light could not have broken forth simultaneously in all parts of the nebula,—that the maximum of heat and of light could scarcely be in the centre of it,—that it might be on its surface, but much more probably was in some spheroidal shell intermediate between the two,—and also that both the light and the heat would be greater in the polar than in the equatorial regions. The reasons on which these conclusions rest are the following:—

[1] Almost all the allowances that have been made are, it will be observed, unfavourable to any exaggeration of the amount of heat produced.

From the dynamical theory of heat, it appears that the increase of heating power acquired by any given molecule in any given time in its descent, would be directly proportional to the attractive force acting upon it, multiplied into the distance through which it descended in that time in obedience to that force. But the distance itself would be directly proportional to the force, and therefore the increase of heating power would be directly proportional to the square of the accelerating force.

It has been proved, in the preceding Note, that, in the case of a spherical nebula at all events, if it were of uniform density, the greatest attractive force would be at the exterior; and there also, consequently, would be the highest temperature and the first dawn of light.[1] But it has also been shown that the great nebula of the solar system could not have been of uniform density, nor of greater density in its exterior than in its interior regions, and consequently must originally have had a higher degree of condensation towards the centre than at greater distances. But there is only one law of distribution of density which could cause an equal augmentation of temperature throughout the whole mass in the same time, and consequently a simultaneous breaking forth of light in every part—that is, when the attractive force towards the centre is the same at all distances; and that could only be when the mass of every concentric sphere of the nebula was proportional to the *square* of the radius, and therefore the density at every point inversely proportional to the distance of that point from the centre. But if such had been the arrangement at first, it could not have continued so, since the density in the parts nearer to the centre would have increased so much more rapidly than in those more distant from it, that the proportion would have been altered immediately. Neither could that law have extended *at any time* as far as the centre, unless

[1] It may be objected that our expressions have changed from *heating power* to temperature; but probably that will make no serious difference. The subject is complicated, and much yet remains for the mathematician to work out.

the density at the centre was infinite. Such, therefore, could not have been the law of distribution throughout the whole mass. Even with a density diminishing towards the exterior, there might have been such a law of that diminution as would have made the light appear first on the exterior surface; but the following considerations will show that to be highly improbable.

However much the nebula may have become compressed as a whole, and however much it may have increased more in density in its interior than in its exterior regions as time advanced, yet we can scarcely conceive that any part of the matter contained in the shells from which the planets were to be aggregated, could pass *through* and *from* these into the interior mass which was afterwards to become the sun. Then, so very small is the whole mass of the planets compared with that of the sun, that we may regard the attractive force of the former, when in its nebulous condition, as so insignificant compared with that of the latter, that we may say that then, as now, *in the planetary regions*, the force of attraction towards the centre was inversely as the square of the distance, very nearly,—a proportion, however, which could not possibly be maintained in the interior and denser part of the nebula. Then, in fact, supposing our view to pass over it towards the centre, after increasing so far it would then diminish, approaching *nothing* as its limit,—so that the greatest attractive force would neither be at the outside nor yet at the centre, but distributed over some shell intermediate between the two, and contained within the central mass; and in that shell would be the greatest heat, and there light would first appear.

It may be said that pressure at the centre would compensate for absence of attractive force; but, as will afterwards appear, it is doubtful if there could be any pressure there, in consequence of the centrifugal force of the surrounding mass; and if there was, it would probably excite very little heat in a mass of solid molecules, and they could not become gaseous until they were heated, nor even then under great pressure. We may therefore conclude that the centre would be the coldest part of the nebula.

I have said, also, that the heat would be greater in the polar than in the equatorial regions. The reason is obvious,—namely, because, since the centrifugal force would cause the nebula to change its form from that of a sphere to that of a spheroid, becoming more and more oblate as its contraction advanced, there would in the course of the change be a greater contraction in its polar than in its equatorial diameter ; and when once the spheroidal form was acquired, the force of gravity also would be greatest near the poles.

NOTE C, Page 53.

Since the footnote on page 53 was written, I find that a systematic attempt has been made to deduce the lengths of the days of all the planets from the nebular hypothesis; and *if that can be done fairly*, it affords the strongest possible confirmation of the truth of that hypothesis. I have not seen the original communication on the subject ; and all that I know of it being from Professor Nichol's *Cyclopædia of the Physical Sciences*, article *Solar System*, I have extracted the passage relating to it from that work :—

'As to the motion of rotation,' in the planets, 'one consideration alone remains worthy of notice. Whence the variety of the periods of this motion ? Why is it that Jupiter performs his rotation in nine hours fifty-six minutes, while the Earth occupies nearly twenty-four hours? Doubtless there is a law at the root of these varieties also; but as yet it has not been clearly discerned. A very ingenious American, however, has recently started an idea meriting all consideration, and by which he attempts to attach these specific periods to the nebular hypothesis. For clearer illustration, imagine the planets all ranged in a straight line from the sun; and let us confine our thoughts to the three bodies, Mars, the Earth, and Venus. It is evident that a point must exist between Venus and the Earth, such that any atom of matter placed in it would be equally attracted towards either of these two orbs; and in the same way, a similar point of indifference could be found between the Earth and Mars. Now the space between these two points may correctly enough be said to be the space which is controlled by the attractive power of the Earth; in other words, an atom, placed anywhere within that space, would—all other conditions being suitable—be drawn from a state of rest towards the Earth, and not either to Venus or Mars. Advancing a step further, a ring, whose breadth is determined by the distance between the foregoing two points, may be supposed to environ the Sun, the Earth's orbit being within it; and this ring may, for manifest reasons, be termed *the sphere of the attraction of the Earth.* Finally, arising in precisely the same manner, every planet may be conceived accompanied by its ring . . .; and these rings may be termed, as in the former case, *the spheres* of attraction of the several globes. . . . "The partition of the original nebula into a number of rings, with such breadths, or nearly such, is perfectly consistent with the fact that the said rings have ultimately resolved themselves into planets of the relative order and magnitude distinguishing those now existing." Not only is this new supposition not hostile to the general tenor of the nebular hypothesis; but, on the contrary, it is altogether consistent and congruous with it.—We reach the remarkable and conclusive result. Mr. Kirkham, of Pennsylvania, who first started the idea of these spheres of attraction, has found in them the periods of the rotations of the several planets. The law announced by him is this: "The square of the number of times that each planet rotates during one revolution in its orbit, is proportional to the cube of the breadth, or diameter, of its sphere of attraction."'

I will not stop to inquire how far the above is consistent with other views which I have attempted to give of the contraction of the nebula. The subject is complicated and difficult. The fact is, that the development of the nebular hypothesis throws open an extensive field for computations of all kinds.

Mr. Herbert Spencer, in one of his *Essays*, has brought forward several new arguments in support of Laplace's hypothesis; but they require further examination than they have yet received before their testimony can be relied upon.

NOTE D, Page 54.

One of the authors of the well-known *Essays and Reviews* [1] says: 'That the Hebrews understood the sky, firmament, or heaven to be a permanent solid vault, is evident enough from various expressions made use of concerning it. It is said to have pillars (Job xxvi. 11), foundations (2 Sam. xxii. 8), doors (Ps. lxxviii. 23), and windows (Gen. vii. 11).'

As to the first three of these quotations, they are all from the midst of descriptions highly poetical; and if we are to take one expression literally, we must take others also contiguous to it. In the case of the passage first quoted, two verses almost immediately preceding it—namely, the seventh and eighth—demolish the Essayist's notion : 'He stretcheth out the north over an empty place, and hangeth the earth upon nothing. He bindeth up the water in his thick clouds; and the cloud is not rent under them.' The north would not be stretched over an empty place if it rested on solid pillars standing on firm foundations; and in the latter verse, instead of the water of the clouds being conceived to rest on a glassy vault, it is spoken of as enclosed in a skin bottle which is strong enough to hold it without bursting. Would any reader in his senses take that literally? In the case of Gen. vii. 11, the word *windows* is rendered in the margin *floodgates,* and what reason have we for taking either the one or the other of these as anything more than a figurative expression?

No doubt the Hebrew word for firmament, namely *rakiah,* is derived, as we are told, from the verb *rakah,* which means *to spread metal thin with the hammer;* but this conveys the idea of extent rather than of solidity. Any one in quest of a material figure to represent solidity would be more likely to

---

[1] Mr. Goodwin, in *Mosaic Cosmogony,* p. 220.

select a mass of iron than a sheet of gold leaf. But admitting both meanings to be possible, judging from the etymology alone, it is surely allowable to select that which appears the more reasonable, or the more likely to be the sense in which it was understood by the writer. Now, had our Essayist read the whole of the chapter carefully (for it is the first chapter of Genesis on which he is commenting), he would have come to the twentieth verse, in which we read of 'fowl that may fly abroad in the open firmament of heaven.' Birds certainly could not fly in a solid vault. The writer might say, perhaps (although he does not say so), that we have in the margin another translation of this clause, namely, 'fowl that may fly above the earth, in the face of the firmament of heaven;' but assuredly, if Moses believed the firmament to be a solid vault, he knew that it was elevated far above all the mountain-tops on which he had fed his flocks in Arabia ; and it certainly would not have been natural on the part of one having that knowledge, to say that the birds were flying in the face of such a vault, when they were almost all thousands of feet below it.

Again, in very many passages of the Bible we read of 'the fowls of heaven;'[1] and in others again, exactly similar, of the fowls or birds of the air,[2] clearly identifying the words *air* and *heaven*, or at least taking them as synonymous as far as the air extended. And as if to make the matter still more clear, we have in the Apocalypse (xix. 17), 'All the fowls that fly in the midst of heaven.'

Even if we were to assign to the word *rakiah* the idea of a solid expanse, in as far as the etymology of the word is concerned—for undoubtedly the idea of 'crystalline spheres' did appear at one time among the ancients ; and if we were to admit that such might have been the sense *originally* attached to the word, it would by no means follow that *Moses* used the word in that sense, any more than that Addison used the corresponding English word in that sense, when he spoke of

[1] Gen. vii. 23 and ix. 2; Job xxviii. 21 and xxxv. 11; Ps. lxxix. 2 and civ. 12; Jer. vii. 33, xvi. 4 ; etc.
[2] Gen. ii. 9 and vii. 3; Ps. viii. 8 ; and Deut. xxviii. 26.

'the spacious *firmament* on high,' or that modern astronomers use it in that sense when they speak of ' our own *firmament* of stars,' as distinguished from other stellar systems. The etymology of the English word certainly conveys the idea of *solidity* as decidedly as any Hebrew word can do, and yet writers of our own day use it when there can be no suspicion of such a belief, and when we certainly have a greater abundance of scientific words to choose from than Moses could possibly have had. If Macaulay's hypothetical New Zealander should dig an old poem of the nineteenth century out of the ruins of the British Museum, and read in it of a certain lady's 'bewitching smile,' and then, returning to his own island, should attempt to hold *that* up to his fellow-countrymen as a proof that at the date of the poem the English believed in witchcraft, he would, I apprehend, make a blunder of the same kind as that which Mr. Goodwin has fallen into. There is no reason why Moses should not have used old words in a new sense, just as we use them.

NOTE E, Page 57.

In a memoir of Hugh Miller, prefixed to the last edition of his *Footprints of the Creator*, and written partly by Professor Agassiz, partly by Sir David Brewster, we have the following remark, probably from the pen of the latter. Speaking of the *development hypothesis*, he says : ' Driven by the discoveries of Lord Rosse from the domain of astronomy, where it once seemed to hold a plausible position, it might have lingered with the appearance of life among the ambiguities of the palæozoic formations ; but Mr. Miller has stripped it even of its semblance of truth.' Probably Sir David viewed the nebular hypothesis only in the light of its fancied opposition to revelation, and was therefore prejudiced against it; but something more, perhaps, might have been expected of him than to confound it with the development hypothesis of Lamarck, with which it has in reality no connection. The latter holds out, not that every individual animal has been developed through the successive stages of fœtal life, infancy, youth, and age, but that lower *species* are developed through a succession of individuals into higher. The latter is *a fancy*, which has been thoroughly smashed by the skilfully wielded hammer of Hugh Miller, while the former is an undoubted *fact.* Now it is with the former, the fact, that the nebular hypothesis claims kindred, not with the latter, the fancy. Its subject is the growth of the solar system through the successive stages of nebula and rings, to planets and a solar orb; but the same individual system all the while. Neither does it follow, as Sir David seems to have thought, that although the telescope should succeed in resolving all the nebulæ into separate stars, the nebular hypothesis would therefore fall to the ground. Sir John Herschel has given a more correct view of the subject. He says :[1] 'The more or less advanced state of a nebula towards its segregation into discrete stars, and of these stars themselves towards a denser state of aggregation round a central nucleus, would thus be, in some sort, an indication of age. Neither is there any variety of aspect which nebulæ offer, which stands at all in contradiction to this view. Even though we should feel ourselves compelled to reject the idea of a gaseous or vaporous "nebulous matter," it loses none of its force. Subsidence, and the central aggregation consequent on subsidence, may go on quite as well among a multitude of discrete bodies under the influence of attraction, and feeble or partially opposing projectile motions, as among the particles of a gaseous fluid.'

If, however, it were a point of any consequence, the tables are again turned against those who held Brewster's view of Lord Rosse's observations, by the discovery of actually gaseous nebulæ, and even of the existence of hydrogen gas, in our own sun, by means of the spectroscope.

[1] *Outlines of Astronomy,* third edition, art. 871.

NOTE F, Page 61.

The scene alluded to in the footnote to page 61, is that pre-sented by the great volcano of Kirauea, in Hawaii, the largest of the Sandwich Islands. Its appearance is thus described by Mr. Ellis (who was the first European to visit it) in his inte-resting *Polynesian Researches*, vol. iv. ch. x.:—

'After walking some distance over the sunken plain, which in several places sounded hollow under our feet, we at length came to the edge of the great crater, where a spectacle sublime, and even appalling, presented itself before us. We stopped and trembled. Astonishment and awe for some moments rendered us mute; and, like statues, we stood fixed to the spot, with our eyes riveted on the abyss below. Immediately before us yawned an immense gulf, in the form of a crescent, about two miles in length from north-east to south-west, nearly a mile in width, and apparently eight hundred feet deep. The bottom was covered with lava, and the south, west, and northern parts of it were one vast flood of burning matter, in a state of terrific ebullition, rolling to and fro its fiery surge and flaming billows. Fifty-one conical islands of varied form and size, containing as many craters, rose either round the edge or from the surface of the burning lake. Twenty-two constantly emitted columns of grey smoke, or pyramids of brilliant flame; and several of these at the same time vomited from their ignited mouths streams of lava, which rolled in blazing torrents down their black indented sides into the boiling mass below.'

Mr. Ellis afterwards describes the same scene by night:—

'Between nine and ten, the dark clouds and heavy fog that, since the setting of the sun, had hung over the volcano, gradually cleared away; and the fires of Kirauea, darting their fierce light across the midnight gloom, unfolded a sight ter-rible and sublime beyond all we had yet seen.

'The agitated mass of liquid lava, like a flood of melted metal, raged with tumultuous whirl. The lively flame that danced over its undulating surface, tinged with sulphureous blue or glowing with mineral red, cast a broad glare of dazzling light on the indented sides of the insulated craters, whose roaring mouths, amidst rising flames and eddying streams of fire, shot up at frequent intervals, with very loud detonations, spherical masses of fusing lava or bright ignited stones.'

He then proceeds to quote from the narrative of Mr. Stewart, who afterwards visited the volcano along with Lord Byron and a party from the *Blonde* frigate. After a description of the volcano, and an account of a dangerous attempt which they made to cross one corner of the molten lake by walking on the crust which had then hardened over it, the account proceeds:—

'The volcano again began roaring and labouring with redoubled activity. The confusion of noises was prodigiously great. . . . The whole air was filled with the tumult, and those most soundly asleep were quickly roused by it to thorough wakefulness. Lord Byron sprang up in his cot, exclaiming, "We shall certainly have an eruption ; such power must burst through everything!" He had barely ceased speaking when a dense column of heavy black smoke was seen rising from the crater directly in front of us : the subterranean struggle ceased, and immediately after flames burst from a large cone, near which we had been in the morning, and which then appeared to have been long inactive. Red-hot stones, cinders, and ashes were also propelled to a great height with immense violence ; and shortly after the molten lava came boiling up, and flowed down the sides of the cone, and over the surrounding scoriæ, in two beautiful curved streams, glittering with indescribable brilliance.

'At the same time a whole lake of fire opened in a more distant part. This could not have been less than two miles in circumference, and its action was more horribly sublime than anything I ever imagined to exist, even in the ideal visions of unearthly things. Its surface had all the agitation of an ocean : billow after billow tossed its monstrous bosom in the air, and occasionally those from different directions burst with such violence as, in the concussion, to dash the fiery spray thirty and forty feet high. It was at once the most splendidly beautiful and dreadfully fearful of spectacles, and irresistibly turned the thoughts to that lake of fire from whence the smoke of torment ascendeth for ever and ever.'

NOTE G, Page 76.

It has been thought by many, including Fourier and Humboldt, that the central mass of the earth is really in a state of fusion, and that volcanic eruptions are nothing else than the escape of a portion of that liquid mass when partially relieved, at a particular spot, from the superincumbent pressure. It has been shown, however, that the phenomena of precession are not in accordance with the existence of such a bottomless ocean of liquid. It has also been said that, if there were such a melted mass below an outer crust, it would be subject to tides in the same way as the ocean, and these would render the said crust but a crazy and unsteady foundation for our buildings. That objection would be easily answered; but there remains one of a thousand times more weight, and unanswerable. That is,—if the lava of our highest volcanic peaks has been thrown out by the central force, that force, by a law of hydrostatic pressure, could not be exerted on one point of the outer shell without telling equally on every part of it; and such force would be far more than sufficient to lift up the whole superincumbent crust, and break it everywhere, if not blow it into fragments. If, then, the interior is at a temperature sufficient to melt it, and yet is not melted, how can we explain the paradox? Simply thus,—because the enormous pressure retains it in a solid state, although its temperature is such that, if the pressure were removed, it would instantly melt. I think it is Mr. Nasmyth who has shown by experiment what others have inferred from theoretical considerations,—that the temperature of the melting-point of all substances depends on the pressure.

As soon as we make out intense heat to be consistent with solidity, all the objections to a central heat urged by Sir Charles Lyell and others, arising from the fluidity supposed necessarily to accompany it, fall to the ground.

NOTE H, Page 82.

'Recently the transport by ice, and the internal conditions of an Arctic climate, have been suggested by Professor Ramsay as connected with the accumulation of the Permian breccia-conglomerates of Salop and Worcester.   Professor Ramsay, who was the first to advocate in a decided manner the glacial origin of these breccias, founds his belief on the following evidences :—1. The great size of many of the fragments—the largest observed weighing (by a rough estimate) from a half to three-quarters of a ton.   2. Their forms. Rounded pebbles are exceedingly rare.   They are angular or subangular, and have those flattened sides so peculiarly characteristic of many glacier fragments in existing moraines, and also of many of the stones in the Pleistocene drifts, and the moraine matter of the Welsh, Highland, Irish, and Vosges glaciers.   3. Many of them are highly polished, and others are grooved and finely striated like the stones of existing Alpine glaciers, and like those of the ancient glaciers of the Vosges, Wales, Ireland, and the Highlands of Scotland, or like many stones in the Pleistocene drifts.   4. A hardened cementing mass of red marl, in which the stones are very thickly scattered, and which in some respects may be compared to a red boulder clay, in so far that both contain angular, flat-sided, and striated stones, such as form the breccias wherever they occur.'—*Advanced Text-book of Geology*, by David Page, F.G.S., third edition, art. 222.   Dr. Page refers, for his information, to the *Journal of the Geological Society*, vol. xi.

Murchison, no doubt, objects to the idea of glaciers in any but recent times ; but his *arguments* apply only to the Silurian

and older periods, in regard to which, it is unnecessary to say,
I cordially agree with him.

NOTE K, Page 83.

In the remarks on page 83, it is not meant to assert or
imply that, in the Permian age, the earth became, in as far
as its internal temperature is concerned, colder than it is at
present. Far from it! According to our theory it must have
been much hotter; and when the sun's heat came to be added
to that of the earth, we find, according to the testimony of
geologists, that the temperature rose higher in the Secondary
and Tertiary periods than it does in our own day. 'The
Maestricht beds,' says Sir Charles Lyell,[1] 'are classed as the
newest of the Secondary series; and the fossils of that group,
including the remains of gigantic reptiles, indicate the prevalence of a very hot climate.' And again :[2] 'In the deposits of
that period,' the older Tertiary, 'we find the remains of many
animals analogous to those of hot climates, together with
many large shells of the genus *nautilus*, and plants indicating
such a temperature as is found along the southern borders of
the Mediterranean.' All this is exactly what we might expect
as the result of our theory,—a Mediterranean climate in this
latitude in the Tertiary period,—a very hot climate in the
Secondary,—one still more sultry, according to evidence afterwards to be adduced,[3] in the Carboniferous era, and even
hotter than that in the previous ages, but with an icy period
coming between the Carboniferous and the Secondary. The
palæozoic earth slowly but steadily cooled, till, by the time the
Permian system was completed, the vital powers of nature
were all but destroyed. Then the sun shone forth and
gradually restored the temperature, till by the end of the
Secondary it had become not very much lower than it was in

[1] *Principles of Geology*, book i. ch. viii.
[2] *The same*, book i. ch. vi.
[3] See page 86 and Note L.

the Carboniferous era, although with no evidence now of the universal diffusion of an equable temperature. Then it continued to cool till the Tertiary system was completed, exactly as we might expect.

But, it may be said, if the earth itself was very much warmer at the end of the Permian age than it is now, as all that I have said would lead us to infer, would the non-existence of a sun be a sufficient cause for bringing on an icy temperature? When we reflect upon the effect of a single winter's night with a north wind blowing, we may easily imagine what temperature our atmosphere would attain to if we had a perpetual night, perpetual winter, and no warmer winds than those which blow from the north. Even with the ground a little below the surface much warmer than it is now, probably all vegetable and animal life would perish. Even a very high temperature of the earth could not, without a sun, have nursed the luxuriant Carboniferous flora, if radiation had not been prevented by a very humid atmosphere, which we have no reason to believe would continue when the solar rays began to tell upon it.

Not only do the successive changes, which I have here pointed out, in the temperature of the earth harmonize with our hypothesis and its natural results; but the present conditions of the sun, the moon, and the earth, all add their testimony to the same effect. They are all exactly as we should expect them to be if our theory is correct. The smallest of these, the moon, is so much cooled down, that even its volcanoes, once very numerous, are extinct; the earth, considerably larger, is cool on the surface, but hot beneath; while the sun, incomparably the largest, is also incomparably the hottest, not having as yet made an approach to coolness even on the surface. Notwithstanding its great bulk, the sun could not have remained so hot on the exterior if it had been solid; but undoubtedly its outer shell at all events is in a melted condition, lower strata rising successively to the surface as the upper are cooled, but none of them attaining a solid condition on the surface.

K

NOTE L, Page 87.

Sir Charles Lyell confirms the authority of Sir Roderick Murchison in regard to the prevalence, during the formation of the Carboniferous and previous systems, of a very warm temperature in the higher latitudes. After some remarks (partly quoted in Note K) on the high temperature of the Secondary and Tertiary ages, he says:[1] 'But it is from the more ancient coal deposits that the most extraordinary evidence has been supplied in proof of the former existence of an extremely hot climate in those latitudes which are now the temperate and colder regions of the globe. It appears from the fossils of the Carboniferous period, that the flora consisted almost exclusively of large vascular cryptogamic plants. We learn from the labours of M. Ad. Brogniart, that there existed at that epoch *Equiseta* upwards of ten feet high and from five to six inches in diameter ; tree ferns, or plants allied to them, from forty to fifty feet in height ; and arborescent *Lycopodiacea* from sixty to seventy feet high. Of the above classes of vegetables the species are all small at present in cold climates, while in tropical regions there occur, together with small species, many of a much greater size ; but their development, even in the hottest parts of the globe, is now inferior to that indicated by the petrified forms of the coal formation. An elevated and uniform temperature, and great humidity of the air, are the causes most favourable to the numerical predominance and the great size of these plants within the torrid zone at present.' Sir Charles adds in another place :[2] 'The uninjured corals and chambered univalves of Iglooik, Melville Island, and other high latitudes, sufficiently prove that during the Carboniferous period there was an elevated temperature even in northern regions bordering on the Arctic Circle. *The heat and humidity of the air and the uniformity of climate*

[1] *Principles of Geology*, book i. ch. vi.
[2] *Ibid.* book i. ch. vi.

appear to have been most remarkable when the oldest strata hitherto discovered were formed.' The italics are my own, as I wish to draw attention to the remarkable confirmation it gives to our hypothesis, and that, I may say, unintentionally; for Sir Charles has another theory of his own, by which he endeavours to explain the great heat of certain periods, and the equally great cold of others. His theory is this : that the heat and cold not only of particular regions, but of the whole globe, depend materially upon the distribution of land and sea. The first part of this proposition is at once conceded, but the other part I deny altogether. We may set it down as an established truth, that no change of any probable or even possible kind, in the extent, shape, or position of the continents and islands of the earth, would affect its *average temperature* in the slightest degree. No doubt the air and the ocean, between them, are the great means provided for the equalization of the earth's temperature, or, more correctly speaking, for moderating the extremes of heat and cold which would be the result of the sun's influence if it were not counterbalanced by some means. *But* for these, the tropical and the arctic regions would be alike uninhabitable. By far the greater part of that useful work of equalization is undoubtedly performed by the air, as we see from the winds that are constantly blowing everywhere, over both land and sea, unrestrained by limits, and consequently attaining to high velocities. Their temperature also is sometimes very much above that of the regions towards which they are blowing. The currents of the ocean, on the other hand, are constantly turned aside and checked by the interfering lands, so that they rarely attain a velocity of more than two or three miles per hour : they extend over only a part of the earth's surface, not only the land being excluded, but all the smaller seas and confined bays; and their temperature is, I think, never more than a few degrees ahead of that of the region through which they are travelling, the only compensation to this arising from the high specific heat of water. But granting the utmost capability that any one chooses to claim for the cooling and heating power of the ocean currents, still it must always be remembered that they are only equalizers of heat : they produce none, and destroy none ;[1] they add to the warmth of the polar regions only by robbing the equatorial, and they cannot affect the *average* temperature of the earth to the extent of a single degree. Now all testimony concurs in establishing the fact that, in the Carboniferous era, there was a tropical climate from the equator to at least the latitude of Melville Island, and probably therefore from pole to pole ; and, according to Sir Charles' own admission already quoted, the heat and the humidity of the air appear to have been still more remarkable in the previous periods.

Sir Charles decries hypothesis ; but is it not a pure hypothesis that the land and water of the globe were ever distributed in either of the two ways he exhibits in his diagram? No doubt it is *possible* that they were so ; but is it probable that they would continue in any such peculiar condition during the immensely long palæozoic period, including, without going further back, the Silurian, the Devonian, and the Carboniferous systems, and that, too, notwithstanding the terrible overturnings which we know took place during the time?

He is not satisfied, however, with the hypothetical adjustment of the ocean to serve the purpose required, but calls to its aid the mountains, the clouds, and the snow.

First, as to the *mountains.* He says :[2] 'The elevated land rising to the colder regions of the atmosphere becomes a great reservoir of ice and snow,—arrests, condenses, and congeals vapour, and communicates its cold to the adjoining country.' Consequently, if our highest mountains were reduced in elevation, he infers, the temperature of the globe would be increased ; for he continues in another passage :[3] 'If we suppose that, at certain periods, no chain of hills in the world rose beyond the height of 10,000 feet, a greater heat might then have prevailed than is consistent with the existence of mountains of thrice

[1] That which appears to be lost in evaporation or in liquefaction is only rendered latent ; and that which is converted into motive power is no exception, since it is at any time reconvertible into heat.

[2] *Principles of Geology*, book i. ch. vii.   [3] *Ibid.* book i. ch. vii.

that elevation.' In reply to this, we may say that it has now been proved[1] that the mountains, even the highest, do not cool the subjacent land, but warm it: for, as to their 'condensing and congealing vapour,' that produces heat, not cold; as to radiation, however cold they may be themselves, they are warmer than the clouds or sky above them; and as to their cooling the winds which pass over them, as is commonly fancied, it is the winds that cool them, and not they that cool the winds. The wind, as it rises towards their summits, is cooled by expanding, but regains all its warmth as it descends, with that derived from condensation and congelation of vapour added to it. The effect of elevations on the *average* temperature of the globe is simply *nothing*.

Clouds are in exactly the same position. If they prevent the earth beneath from being directly heated by the sun's rays, they receive the heat themselves, and ultimately impart it to the earth. Nothing more can be said for *snow*. If it reflects almost all the rays of the sun which fall on it, so we may say it equally reflects the cold of the sky. If it absorbs little of the sun's radiated heat, so it in its turn radiates equally little to the atmosphere. All that snow effects is to preserve the temperature of the underlying surface of the ground *in statu quo*, preventing heat from passing either in or out.

The sum of all this is, that, setting aside the warmth supplied from within, so long as the heat of the sun is constant, the average temperature of the earth's surface is constant, however the balance may be disturbed in its different parts. No solar ray enters our atmosphere in vain.

Sir Charles Lyell certainly never professes to show that any distribution of land and sea could do anything more than produce a temperature throughout the greater part of the earth's surface approaching to the present heat of our tropical regions. He nowhere suggests that it could be higher than that, unless in some peculiar localities. It could not *generally* be so high,

[1] See a communication in the *Transactions of the Literary and Philosophical Society of Liverpool* for 1859, 'On the Causes of Local Peculiarities of Temperature.'

even on his own hypothesis, as to be unfavourable to vegetation. Then how can we account for the almost perfect steri-
lity of the earth during the earlier palæozoic periods, with no
vegetation whatever known in the Laurentian and Cambrian
eras, and no animal life in the former except that one little
creature the Eozöon Canadense, and in the latter nothing
higher than a few zoophytes? If vegetable and animal life
were the results of a happy concourse of atoms afterwards ·
improved by adaptation to circumstances, here was time enough
for every chance to come into operation, and yet life remained
undeveloped. But if, as we believe, plants and animals required creative power for their production, is it likely that an
all-wise Creator would leave the earth so long a desert if it
had been in a fit state for being clothed with vegetation and
peopled with animals? We hear a kind of explanation in the
hypothesis that the older strata were all deposited in deep
seas; but as no geologist, I think, now holds the old doctrine
of a ' primeval universal ocean,' the seas, however deep, must
have had shores and shallow bays, and it is only near the
shores that deposits of sand and clay are made. Besides that,
the Lower Silurian rocks, as far as my own observation goes,
show no traces of any deep sea whatever, but many of shallow
pools and muddy plains. If, however, the earth was, as we
have supposed, during the earlier palæozoic ages, at a temperature closely approaching to boiling heat, all things are
consistent.

'There are no proofs,' says the great geologist so often
quoted in this note,[1] ' of a secular decrease of heat accompanied by contraction. On the contrary, Laplace has shown,
by reference to astronomical observations made in the time of
Hipparchus, that in the last two thousand years there has
been no sensible contraction of the globe by cooling; for had
this been the case, even to an extremely small amount, the
day would have been shortened, whereas its length has certainly not diminished during that period.' This is granted;

---

[1] *Principles of Geology,* book i. ch. viii.

but Sir Charles has fallen into a mistake common to geologists, in fancying that cooling necessarily involves contraction. It does so certainly when the cooling is unaccompanied by change of condition; but when any melted matter, in cooling, changes from the liquid to the solid state, it almost always expands. One stratum of the globe would therefore expand in cooling, while others would contract; and the result of the two effects united might be no perceptible change in the diameter of the earth, or in the length of the day, if two thousand years is not too short a period to render the result perceptible according to any way of taking it.

If the earth must now be in the same condition in which it has always been, why not apply the same principle to the moon? But, unfortunately for the argument of the uniformitarians, we have the moon's history written in its face so clearly, that 'he that runs may read.' It has at one time been covered with active volcanoes, and these are now either entirely at rest, or so nearly so, that, if some have thought they saw a speck of conflagration still lingering, it is never very clear whether it was a fact or a fancied appearance.

NOTE M, Page 88.

In the fourth chapter I have said that, if the sun made its appearance in our world for the first time during the fourth day, it might have been expected that some vestiges of the great change would be found in the fossil remains of that period ; and accordingly such vestiges are found very clearly, —first, in a complete renovation of the whole animal and vegetable creation at that period ; and secondly, in a change from a flora and fauna which showed no distinction of climates, to one in which the productions of the tropical regions were altogether distinct from those of the higher latitudes. To these evidences of the important change in the source from which the heat of the earth's surface was mainly supplied, a third has been added, still more decided, if possible, than

these, provided that it could be clearly established. It has
been said that season-rings, such as are seen in the timber of
all the forest trees of our own country, showing the alterna-
tions of summer and winter, are not to be found in the fossil
remains of any trees which grew previously to the Triassic
formations. Other writers, however, inform us that exogenous
trees, showing similar rings, did exist previously to that era ;
and if it could be fairly established that the rings seen in
these were truly annual, their formation must have been dependent upon the sun, and would go far towards proving that
the sun's first appearance must have been at an earlier period
than has been assigned to it in this volume. It is a point of
very great importance, which has not yet been sufficiently
investigated. The probable solution of the difficulty seems to
be, that although, in some few fossil trees of the Carboniferous
era, rings may be seen, yet they are not really annual rings.
Rings may appear in plants resembling those in our timber,
and yet not formed in the same way. A hard fungus may be
seen, growing out of the decaying trunks of trees, with rings
exactly resembling those of a tree, and equally perfect ; but
these are not annual rings. Some fossil plants, supposed to
be fucoid, but with thick stems, are found in the unaltered
Silurian rocks of the south of Scotland, and these stems
sometimes show one or two rings, but with no appearance or
probability of their being season-rings. Professor Balfour, in
his *Class-book of Botany* (p. 85), says : ' Various peculiarities
occur, especially among exogenous trees of warm climates,
which often obscure the arrangement. Thus, in some trees of
great age, only one marked zone or circle of woody matter is
seen, consisting of a series of separate wedges ; in other trees
there are several such zones, each of which is the produce of
more than one year's growth.' And again, more to the purpose (on p. 81): ' It is said that, in some of the trees of
Tropical America, monthly circles are formed, while in species
of Cactus and Cicas more than one year is required to form
a single zone.' Mr. Miller somewhere informs us that all the
exogenous trees found in the strata antecedent to the Trias

are of species more nearly allied to the Araucaria than to any other modern tree. Now there is something peculiar about the growth of the Araucaria; for to this day it asserts, to a certain extent, its independence of the sun. In Scotland, at all events, if not in warmer climates, its main stem, as well as each branch, puts out a shoot only once in two years, the shoot growing to half its full length the first year, and completing its growth in the second. Now we can scarcely conceive that the formation of the successive rings does not accord with that of the new shoots; and if so, they cannot be annual rings, and consequently cannot be grown in summer and hardened in winter, like those of our common trees. There is therefore some way of forming rings independently of the sun and the seasons, and that, we may suspect, was the mode in which the rings were formed in the pre-triassic timber, judging more especially from their probable relationship. Although, therefore, we cannot, in the present state of our knowledge, use the argument derived from season-rings as decidedly in our favour, yet I think I have said enough to show that it cannot be adduced as decidedly against us. The subject requires further investigation.

Note N, Page 88.

There is a difficulty in this part of our subject connected with *light*. If there was no sun to shed its rays on the earth, can we suppose that the mere light of volcanic fires would be sufficient for the growth of the luxuriant vegetation of the Carboniferous ages? The answer to that will depend upon two things,—the nature of the plants, and the intensity of the volcanic heat. Even with our present vegetation, we are uncertain what amount of light is necessary to its growth. Sir Charles Lyell, in combating the same difficulty, in regard not to volcanic but to solar light, remarks:[1] 'We must bear

[1] *Principles of Geology*, book i. ch. vi.

in mind, in the first place, that, so far as experiments have been made, there is every reason to conclude that the range of intensity of light to which living plants can accommodate themselves is far wider than that of heat. No palms or tree-ferns could live in our temperate latitudes without protection from the cold ; but when placed in hothouses, they grow luxuriantly, even under a cloudy sky, and when much light is intercepted by the glass and framework. At St. Petersburg, in latitude 60° N., these plants have been successfully cultivated in hothouses, although there they must exchange the perpetual equinox of their native regions for days and nights which are alternately protracted to nineteen hours and shortened to five. How much farther towards the pole they might continue to live, provided a due quantity of heat and moisture were supplied, has not yet been determined ; but St. Petersburg is probably not the utmost limit.

'Nor must we forget that we are here speaking of living species formed to inhabit within or near the tropics. But the coal-plants were of perfectly distinct species, and may have been endowed with a different constitution, enabling them to bear a greater variation of circumstances in regard to light. We find that particular species of palms and tree-ferns require at present different degrees of heat, and that some species can thrive only in the immediate neighbourhood of the equator, others only at a distance from it. In the same manner, the minimum of light sufficient for the now existing species cannot be taken as the standard for all analogous tribes that may ever have flourished on the globe.'

Sir Charles adds, in another place (book iii. ch. v.): 'While some plants are covered and uncovered daily by the tide, others live in the abysses of the ocean, at the extraordinary depth of one thousand feet ; and although in such situations there must reign darkness more profound than night, at least to our organs, many of these vegetables are highly coloured.' If, then, aquatic plants can be made to flourish in all but total darkness, there is no reason why land-plants should not have been created adapted to a degree of light far inferior to that of the sun. If eyeless fishes have been created to inhabit dark subterranneous pools, why might not species of plants be produced adapted to lower degrees of light? If it be objected that plants can grow with no light but that of the sun, the fact remains to be proved. The difference between solar and artificial light arises mainly from the difference of temperature of the sources from which they emanate. Then volcanic heat is not artificial heat, but is probably of a kindred character to that of the sun, and may in the earlier ages have glowed with sufficient intensity to support vegetation, especially that of plants adapted to it.

Neither is it certain that the only light of those primeval ages was that which emanated from volcanoes. Auroral light may then have been peculiarly vivid, or light from sources of which we are ignorant.

But should we be in a better position if we gave up volcanic and other auxiliary lights, and resorted to that of the sun for the growth of our coal-plants? The latitude of Melville Island, where coals are found, is 75 degrees, and in winter the sun does not make its appearance there for somewhere about three months. Now, if we could believe that the temperature there, with only the solar heat, would ever be sufficient to grow plants of tropical character, they would remain about three months every winter in nocturnal darkness; and, to quote again the same work : ' Plants, it is affirmed, cannot remain in darkness even for a week without serious injury, unless in a torpid state ; and if exposed to heat and moisture, they cannot remain torpid, but will grow, and must therefore perish. If, then, in the latitude of Melville Island a high temperature and consequent humidity prevailed at that period, when we know the Arctic seas were filled with corals and large multilocular shells, how could plants of tropical forms have flourished, and how could they annually endure a night prolonged for three months?' (Book i. ch. vi.)

No doubt Sir Charles has his own way of endeavouring to extricate himself from this apparently hopeless position; but throughout his whole work he is evidently labouring against

difficulties which he never fairly overcomes, but which are far
more easily surmounted by proceeding on the hypothesis of an
originally very high temperature of the earth.

NOTE O, Page 99.

'In the great series of Secondary rocks, many distinct
assemblies of organized fossils are entombed, all of unknown
species, and many of them referable to genera and families
now most abundant between the tropics. Among the most
remarkable are many gigantic reptiles, some of them herbivorous, others carnivorous, and far exceeding in size any now
known in the torrid zone. The genera are for the most part
extinct; but some of them, as the crocodile and monitor, have
still representatives in the warmer parts of the earth. Coral
reefs also were evidently numerous in the seas of the same
periods, and composed of species belonging to genera now
characteristic of a tropical climate. The number of large
chambered shells also leads us to infer an elevated temperature;
and the associated fossil plants, although imperfectly known,
tend to the same conclusion, the *Cycadea* constituting the most
numerous family.'—*Principles of Geology,* book i. ch. vi.

NOTE P, Page 120.

When this volume was all but completed, I heard for the
first time of an objection, advanced by a French writer, M.
Babinet, to the nebular hypothesis which seems at first sight
formidable. It is this,—that if the rotation of the sun on its
axis is due to the same cause as the revolution of the planets
about the sun, it ought to have been much more rapid than
it is.

It would be very strange, however, if a solitary difficulty like
this were to upset a hypothesis so well supported in such a
variety of ways. It is far more likely that it has some solution

which, although it may not have occurred to the proposer of the objection, and might even entirely evade discovery for the present, may be simple enough. It requires the careful consideration of astronomers; but in the meantime I venture to make some suggestions which may at least serve to show that the difficulty is probably not insuperable.

In the first place, the actual rotatory velocity, even in the outer portions of the nebula, must at first have been very small; and consequently, supposing all parts of the nebula to have rotated in unison, or, in other words, with the same angular velocity, the actual velocity of the matter nearer the centre must have been slower still, in proportion to its distance from the centre. Then, of all the matter which was originally near the centre, the ultimate rotatory velocity would be little more than what was due to the mere shortening of the radius, since it would be very little accelerated by the centripetal force, which, with so little matter between it and the centre, would be very feeble.

In the next place, the same reasoning will be equally applicable to all the matter originally near the axis of rotation, however far it might be from the centre; and all the matter from the polar regions, as Laplace seems to suggest, would necessarily go towards the formation of the sun, that from the outermost of the equatorial zones alone falling into the planets.

Again, we are by no means assured that the molecules, becoming crowded together in the central mass, would not so interfere with each other's movements as to prevent that acceleration of the rotation which would arise from the impetus derived from their fall being turned into the direction of rotation, as was undoubtedly the case with the material of the planets. Such disturbance, as Laplace has proved, could in no way diminish the original rotatory motion; but it might, it seems to me, prevent or diminish its increase from the cause mentioned.

In the fourth place, we have no assurance that all the regions of the nebula did originally rotate in unison. If the angular velocity of rotation was not from the first the same throughout the mass of the nebula, but less and less towards the centre, or even with a reverse motion in the central regions, it would remove the difficulty.

There is another solution of which I cannot see the impossibility, although at first sight it may appear almost fantastical. It involves some considerations of great difficulty, though, if it were once admitted, it would be a key to the explanation of some peculiarities and apparent irregularities in the solar system, which have not yet been explained either by the nebular hypothesis or by any other means. I present it with all diffidence for further consideration.

It is with the revolutions of the planets, not with their rotations, that the rotation of the sun is compared when its slowness is objected to. In the planets we have these two motions separate, while in the sun they are presumed to be united. But is it not possible that they may once have been separated even in the case of the sun, and that we have now only the rotation remaining, the progressive motion being otherwise disposed of? But to show how that might possibly have been, requires explanation.

Suppose, then, that the central mass of the nebula which now constitutes the body of the sun, formed itself in the first place into a ring more or less perfect, as is quite possible and not at all improbable, being only the innermost of the rings formed out of the nebula. Next suppose that ring, by the conjunction of Venus and Mercury, or by any other cause, to have been weakened in one place, and ultimately ruptured on that side, it would slowly draw together towards the opposite side. It would be prevented from collecting in the centre by its own centrifugal force; but when drawn to one side it would gradually lose the restraining centripetal force, and would ultimately fly off into the regions of space.

This motion, compounded with any proper motion which the nebula might have had originally, would result in the proper motion which the sun has now. The velocity of the new progressive motion, being small compared with the velocities of the planets, they would follow in its train, with nothing more than a disturbance of their orbits, changing from a circular to an elliptic form, or, if that change had taken place to some extent before, rendering them more eccentric. Then, if any proper motion which the nebula may have had before was not in the plane of the ecliptic, this new motion of the sun in that plane would also disturb the planes of the orbits of the planets, which would otherwise all have been in one.

But I have entered upon an intricate subject, requiring the acumen of abler mathematicians than I profess to be, and to their consideration I venture to commend it. It may, if thought worthy of being followed out, provide employment for the utmost skill of the rising generation of astronomers. My object is gained if I can show, as I think I have done, that the objection I have been discussing does not form an insuperable obstacle to our reception of the nebular theory. It would have been satisfactory to have had a solution of the difficulty from Laplace himself; but he either did not perceive that it existed, or passed it over in silence.

www.ingramcontent.com/pod-product-compliance
Lightning Source LLC
Chambersburg PA
CBHW020553270326
41927CB00006B/819